ORDERED LIBERTY
AND THE
CONSTITUTIONAL FRAMEWORK

ORDERED LIBERTY
AND THE
CONSTITUTIONAL FRAMEWORK
☆—☆—☆

The Political Thought of Friedrich A. Hayek

Barbara M. Rowland

CONTRIBUTIONS IN POLITICAL SCIENCE, NUMBER 176

GREENWOOD PRESS
NEW YORK • WESTPORT, CONNECTICUT • LONDON

Library of Congress Cataloging-in-Publication Data

Rowland, Barbara Mehl, 1954-
   Ordered liberty and the constitutional framework.

   (Contributions in political science, ISSN 0147-1066 ;
no. 176)
   Bibliography: p.
   Includes index.
   1. Hayek, Friedrich A. von (Friedrich August),
1899-   —Contributions in political science.
I. Title.   II. Series.
JC273.H382R69 1987   320.5'12'0924   87-278
ISBN 0-313-25609-8 (lib. bdg. : alk. paper)

British Library Cataloguing in Publication Data is available.

Library of Congress Catalog Card Number: 87-278
ISBN: 0-313-25609-8
ISSN: 0147-1066

First published in 1987

Greenwood Press, Inc.
88 Post Road West, Westport, Connecticut 06881

Printed in the United States of America

∞

The paper used in this book complies with the
Permanent Paper Standard issued by the National
Information Standards Organization (Z39.48-1984).

10   9   8   7   6   5   4   3   2   1

I dedicate this book with delight to my sons,
Stephen and Benjamin

Contents

viii   Contents

Acknowledgments

I wish to thank John Orbell, critic and friend, for reading several versions of this manuscript; Peregrine Schwartz-Shea, Randy Simmons, Alphons van de Kragt, and Bob and Elaine Lawrence for their moral support; John Gray, who encouraged me to write this book; and John Vloyantes, for his enduring collegiality. A number of the ideas in this book were developed in conversations with Mark Silverstein. The friendship, good humor, and uncompromising commitment to standards of Dean Jaros sustained me at difficult times in the completion of this project. Earlene Bell and Patsy Smith helped with word processing, meeting deadlines, and encouragement, and I am grateful to them.

Receipt of the Dean's Scholarship Support Grant from the College of Arts, Humanities, and Social Sciences at Colorado State University facilitated completion of this project. A special word of thanks goes to my former colleagues in the Department of Political Science at Colorado State University: had it not been for them, I might not have written this book.

Finally, I thank Ruth and Walter Mehl, who helped me create the time and space for writing the initial draft of this book, and Nina Rubin, who taught me about sanity and The Three Musketeers.

ORDERED LIBERTY
AND THE
CONSTITUTIONAL FRAMEWORK

☆ 1 ☆
Introduction: The Paradox
of Evolution and Design

"If old truths are to retain their hold on men's minds,
they must be restated in the language and concepts of
successive generations....It has been a long time since
that ideal of freedom which inspired modern Western
civilization was effectively restated" (1960, p. 1).
Friedrich A. Hayek introduces the body of his book-long
examination of liberty, The Constitution of Liberty,
with this statement of purpose. In this study of
Hayek's political philosophy, I take Hayek at his word,
and examine his thought from the perspective of what he
tells us is his overriding concern, individual liberty.
Despite the richness and complexity of his treatment of
individual liberty, I conclude that his theory of
individual liberty is incoherent, resting upon
fundamental ambiguities in his concept of the self.
After exploring those ambiguities and the insights they
generate, I argue for an expanded understanding of
liberty and suggest new directions for a philosophy of
individual liberty.

In an intellectual career spanning sixty years,
Nobel prizewinner Friedrich Hayek has established
himself as a defender of individual liberty and a
liberal social order. As an economist of the Austrian
school, his contributions to economic theory have
received considerable attention. Despite the return by
political scientists in recent years to a discussion of
basic ideas of political philosophy, Hayek's political
theory has not received much attention; his political
philosophy has been dismissed as that of a reactionary.
As I believe this study clearly demonstrates, this lack
of attention is unwarranted. Hayek's political
philosophy represents a profound effort to solve a
problem which has long preoccupied political thinkers:
how a society can protect individual liberty while
providing for social order.

As a social and political theorist Hayek reflects

upon what a "good society" should look like. The
central elements in his vision, as in the visions of
other philosophers, are liberty and order, which
together imply a just society in the eyes of the people
living within it. How exactly are daily affairs in
such a society to be ordered, so that neither liberty
nor social order is lost?

The proper beginning point in our search for the
answer to that question, according to Hayek, is in
classical liberal theory. The central insight of that
theory is that the actions of free individuals,
provided certain legal, institutional, and moral
requirements are met, can be coordinated in a
decentralized and minimally coercive way that will
provide for the general interest in order of the
society as a whole. There are four tenets of classical
liberal theory which Hayek notes:

1.   the coordination of individual actions can be
     accomplished through spontaneous, decentralized
     mechanisms like the market;
2.   such coordination of individual actions does not
     require shared convictions on ends;
3.   given such coordination, the role for the
     governmental organization need not be large;
4.   proper institutional and legal frameworks for such
     coordination have been achieved through devices
     such as constitutional limits of power and the
     separation of powers.

This classical liberal solution, Hayek contends, should
be regarded as a reasoned judgement drawn from careful
scrutiny of the centuries of human experience from
which Western civilization developed.

He argues that once certain self-evident
propositions about human knowledge are acknowledged,
then the classical liberal solution to the problem of
liberty and order becomes both a reasonable as well as
optimal choice. A full understanding of the classical
liberal solution requires explicit attention to a
series of social institutions which make the
decentralized coordination of the market possible. In
other words, the market institution itself rests upon
other institutions--morals, law, money--whose gradual
development over time has made the market a
freedom-enhancing mechanism. To the extent that
government organizations have become involved in the
preservation and even perhaps the alteration of
supporting social institutions for the market, the
structure of government becomes similarly vital for the
existence of the market as a solution for the problem
of liberty and order.

From an early point in his career, Hayek believed

that the market order and the liberty it embodied, fundamental bases for the continued prosperity and development of Western civilization, was under attack. He has maintained throughout the decades of his work that the attack is devastating in large part because the attackers claim they too are interested in achieving the goals of liberty and order. This belief led him to specify the most important and persistent threats to the market order in twentieth-century Western democracies. The first threat, which Hayek emphasized early in his work, is "planning." His rejection of planning rests on his definition of central planning as a rationalist endeavor to replace a society in which social outcomes are generated by essentially unpredictable and decentralized processes with a society in which social outcomes are to reflect centrally conceived and directed design.

The second threat, also requiring state direction, is what Hayek sees as the effort to achieve economic equality, which he calls the quest for "social justice." Social justice, he contends, is attractive because it caters to an instinctive longing for a sense of community in modern man. The call for planning and for social justice, when adopted in Western democracies, has led to extensive legislation intended to manipulate the market order. Such manipulation, he charges, violates individual liberty and threatens the ability of the market to serve as a decentralized coordinating mechanism.

Legislation aimed at interfering with the market and individual lives is to be regarded as inevitable, given the contemporary structure of representative institutions in Western democracies. This structure as a threat to the market order is emphasized by Hayek in much of his later work. He points out that unintended results of liberal constitutional design have led to institutionalized corruption and vote-trading. In Hayek's presentation, the outcome of logrolling cannot be "efficient" in any sense. This conclusion follows from his understanding of the proper role of a key political structure, the legislature, in a free, market society.

Legislatures are to formulate general, just rules of conduct that provide a supporting framework for moral behavior on the part of individuals in a decentralized market-ordered society. Such enforceable rules of conduct supplement (but do not replace) morals as such, which Hayek regards as one of the key socially evolved products which facilitate "ordered liberty." This is the term I will use to designate Hayek's expanded formulation of the classical liberal conception of individual liberty. In contemporary democratic legislatures, the set of incentives to which legislators respond is far more likely to generate particular measures on which majority coalitions can readily be formed. Two consequences follow, both of which are damaging to the preservation of liberty and order. First, legislative rules of conduct are no longer general in nature and cannot be legitimated as just on that basis. Second, direct interference in the market order becomes routine, setting precedents for more and more intrusion into individual spheres of liberty.

The conclusion Hayek draws from these observations, given his devotion to the ideal of ordered liberty, is that reform of democratic legislatures, via constitutional design, is needed. This conclusion, however, when juxtaposed with Hayek's examination of the limits of human reason and the wisdom of the products of cultural evolution contained in traditions and surviving social institutions, results in a central inconsistency in his thought.

In his discussion of phenomena such as law, morals, and the market, Hayek distinguishes between a spontaneous order and a designed order. Spontaneous orders evolve, reflecting many human actions, but not representing the conscious handiwork of individual reason or governmental plan. The interactions of many individuals generate ordered outcomes because of, rather than in spite of, the absence of planning. The success of such orders and their accompanying institutions is evaluated over time by a process of cultural selection based on the (relative) success of groups of individuals whose pursuit of individual purposes is facilitated by their social institutions. Traditions and institutions which prevail do so because they are conducive to the survival of large groups of people upon which civilization is based.

How then does Hayek evaluate prevailing political institutions? On what basis is he prepared to replace surviving democratic structures with a newly designed set, the specifications of which he himself has outlined? If existing political institutions reflect evolved wisdom, then Hayek's own judgements as to their success or failure seem presumptuous, unless he has a special insight into the process of evolution. He appears to contradict his own call for social scientists to examine particular traditions and institutions with care and respect. Yet he invests his time in devising an admittedly utopian design for a liberal democratic constitution.

To summarize the inconsistency, we can say that on the one hand, Hayek advocates allowing the free growth of society to continue by avoiding the temptation to substitute humanly designed institutions for the products of cultural evolution we may only imperfectly

understand. On the other hand, he seems to disregard
his own warning about the perils of design by offering
a detailed plan for the design of a new democratic
order.

Are these apparently contradictory elements in his
thought indicative of a logical inconsistency in his
philosophy of liberty? This is the question I address
in the pages that follow. If the inconsistency is real
rather than apparent, then Hayek's philosophy, despite
individually valuable elements, will seem little more
than an unsuccessful and internally flawed attempt to
resurrect a dying tradition of liberal thought.

Indeed, a number of Hayek's most penetrating
critics find it difficult to avoid precisely this
conclusion. Norman Barry argues that Hayek's emphasis
on traditionalism poses an insurmountable problem for
his philosophy. "Fundamentally, the problem is that
the anti-rationalism and traditionalism of his general
philosophy is so strong that it virtually disables him
from that critical rationalism which is essential for
the appraisal of particular traditions" (1984, p. 280).
John Gray (1986) similarly concludes that Hayek is
unable to tell us when theoretical insights are to take
precedence over our fund of tacit understanding. This
conflict is at the very center of Hayek's philosophy,
Gray maintains, endangering the unity of Hayek's work.

I will argue in this book that attaining a full
understanding of Hayek's commitment to ordered liberty,
and then applying it to the inconsistent elements in
his thought provides only a partial remedy for the
inconsistency. Such an approach involves regarding his
advocacy of respect for tradition, design for specific
purposes, and rejection of rational constructivism as
secondary concerns whose content must be evaluated in
reference to his principle of liberty. His
constitutional design, I contend, is not inconsistent
with his attack on constructivist rationalism once the
nature of that attack is correctly understood. But his
vision of ordered liberty fails to clarify for us when
design rather than respect, and vice versa, is to be
our goal. In other words, the broader issue of the
relationship between tacit and theoretical knowledge
remains unresolved.

I view this fundamental uncertainty in Hayek's
work as rooted in a confusion about the nature of the
individual or essential self. He moves between two
distinct understandings of the meaning of
individualism. Most of the time, Hayek writes about
the self in a manner consistent with the social
contract theory of individualism initiated by Hobbes.
"Liberal political theory, from Hobbes onward, called
on each citizen to view himself as primarily a
distinct, autonomous atom, unlinked to his fellow atoms

unless he contracts to join them" (Midgley 1983, p.
519). In Hayek's variation on the atomistic mode of
individualism, individuals operate largely on the basis
of rational, or broadly speaking, theoretical
knowledge. These are the individuals "at home" in the
marketplace, responding to abstract price signals
rather than according to perceptions of the needs of
people around them. When Hayek is writing in this
mode, he speaks in Hobbesian fashion of how people
employ knowledge to enhance their chances of
self-preservation.

The exclusive focus on the sole aim of
self-preservation which lies behind many philosophers'
social contract theories has resulted in an exaggerated
picture of individualism as selfish, greedy, and
competitive. This exclusive focus "shrinks the
essential self to a wizened old nut, a bare
intellectual center of choice, unattached to particular
people and things, and equally capable--if its one
abstract need is met--of living anywhere" (Midgley
1983, p. 529).

Hayek expresses another understanding of
individuality, however, especially when he focuses on
tacit knowledge and cultural tradition. When he writes
in this second vein, individuals are presented as
fundamentally social in character, dependent on the
social context of their lives for their reason, their
morality, and their own unique expression of
individuality. While selfhood is celebrated as the
expression of autonomy and responsibility, there is
implicit recognition that each individual
simultaneously must "bear his part in a tremendous
orchestra which existed before he was born and over
which he can never have more than a limited control"
(Midgley 1983, p. 531).

These two ways of viewing the individual I
identify in Hayek's thought are explicitly addressed by
the contemporary communitarian critique of liberalism.
In the terms of that critique, the individual of the
social contract tradition is an "unencumbered self"
(Sandel 1982), a self able to stand at a distance and
choose its values and preferences. Such an individual,
who appears most often as subject in Hayek's philosophy
is by definition ill-equipped to appreciate tradition,
let alone recognize the intrinsic role tradition plays
in rational choice. The individual who is presented as
more social in nature is the "situated self" (MacIntyre
1984), a self whose identity is partly derived from the
traditions of culture but never wholly determined by
them. This kind of individual is by definition
predisposed to understand Hayek's complex vision of the
roles played by tradition and human reason in human
society. Because Hayek himself never completely

succeeds in presenting the self as a situated self, but remains constrained by the paradigm of the unencumbered self, he does not present a unified and coherent philosophy of individual liberty. Instead, he becomes increasingly pessimistic about the future of Western civilization.

The ambiguity in Hayek's thought about the nature of the self is clearly revealed by his treatment of the unencumbered self as an "author" capable of designing plans for its life. For even as he discusses individuals as authors, and their liberty as authors, he persistently describes them making choices within the context of and in response to the rules of tacit knowledge. They become, in Hayek's own account, more "co-authors" than authors (much to the dismay and confusion of some of his critics). It is as though, by remaining locked within the paradigm of the unencumbered self, he falls victim to the rationalist (and indeed constructivist rationalist) hubris he denounces, despite his appreciation for the cultural and traditional bases upon which human reason is built. Even as he denounces the belief in the limitless capacity of human reason to create a brave new world, he laments the failure of the unencumbered self to perceive the connectedness on which its freedom is built. He relies, in effect, on an appeal for unencumbered individuals to recognize that the survival of Western civilization depends upon retaining connections to the traditions from which it emerged. Yet Hayek can have little basis for belief that the appeal will be heard, as his pessimism indicates. The result is an incoherent philosophy of liberty, in which the role of human agency is never clarified.

The breadth and passion of Hayek's work both conceals this confusion and makes it initially plausible to classify him as an "epic theorist," following Sheldon Wolin's use of the term. An epic philosopher responds to a crisis he perceives in the world around him. The theories developed in response to the crisis often "have reflected a conviction...that political action might destroy certain civilized values and practices" (1969, p. 1080). The theorist identifies a "systematic derangement" in "arrangements, in decisions, and in beliefs." To do this, the theorist must point to basic principles which produce the derangement.

There is another central element present in the work of epic theorists, Wolin suggests. They present a picture of an ordered whole which is contrasted with the systematic derangement they critique. At this point, I argue, the effort to classify Hayek as an epic theorist must fail. For it is in the alternative he seeks to offer that the limitations of his political

philosophy become apparent. His vision of liberty,
like the vision of the self upon which it rests,
despite a number of intriguing and promising elements,
is too narrow to serve as an alternative basis for
envisioning change in contemporary liberal societies.
     The development of a new direction for liberal
theory can gain a great deal from study of Hayek's
philosophy, despite its ultimate confusion. For he
introduces important insights about the social nature
of ordered liberty even if he fails to incorporate them
into a coherent concept of the self. Hayek's peculiar
contribution, then, is that he unknowingly reveals the
dilemmas liberal theory confronts if the unencumbered
self is assumed to describe the liberal actor. When we
supplement the image of the self with attention to the
concept of the situated self, however, I suggest that
new directions in a philosophy of liberty can be
discovered.   An outline of what those new directions,
and the resultant new philosophy might look like, is
offered in my concluding chapter.
     I begin my discussion of the insights and limits
of Hayek's philosophy in the second chapter with an
examination of his skeptical epistemology and critical
rationalism.   I show how his epistemology informs his
distinction between constructivist and critical
rationalism, specifying the nature of his attack on
constructivist rationalism and explaining why his
constitutional design is consistent with that attack.
I complete my exploration of his application of
critical rationality by looking carefully at his
constitutional proposals, and assessing the ways in
which they are similar to those of James Madison.
     In the third chapter, Hayek's view of the
evolution of civilization is examined, in order to
facilitate understanding how his view of the self leads
him into a deepening pessimism about human agency and
an accompanying blind faith in the forces of cultural
evolution.   His views on cultural evolution are
compared with those of another thoughtful social
scientist, psychologist Donald Campbell.   I conclude
that Hayek's failure to accord a role to critical
reason in the daily assessment and transformation of
norms of behavior is the driving force behind his
embrace of conservatism in recent years.
     In the fourth chapter, I consider alternatives to
my argument that the most appropriate way to understand
the role of Hayek's proposals for constitutional reform
in the context of the whole of his writings is to see
them as a reflection of his view of ordered liberty.   I
formulate three competing explanations by which the
presence of his constitutional design and his
traditionalism can be understood.   These explanations
are: that his constructivist constitutionalism is a

result of confused terminology complicated by
contradictory philosophical preferences; that his
design is a product of his preoccupation with the goal
of human progress; and that his proposals reflect his
unwavering commitment to a free market society. I
argue that the textual evidence as a whole does not
support these explanations but points to the validity
of my perspective. Hayek's constitutional proposals
are driven by and derived from his complex definition
of ordered liberty.

I give that definition full consideration in
chapter five. I detail its central focus on limits and
the relationship between discipline and freedom for the
individual. After exploring the place of Hayek's view
of liberty in contemporary political philosophy, the
parallels of Hayek's resultant philosophy of justice
with a Rawlsian perspective are established. Sandel's
communitarian critique of Rawls is then applied to
Hayek's work to focus our attention once more on the
nature of the self presumed in Hayek's understanding of
ordered liberty.

In the final chapter, I offer an assessment of
Hayek's philosophy of liberty, examining the extent to
which he shares insights with conservative and
communitarian critics of liberalism. His vision of the
role of community in liberal society is compared to
that of Nozick and MacIntyre. I conclude with a
proposal for a revised understanding of the meaning of
ordered liberty for the individual based upon a fuller,
richer conception of the "essential self."

☆ 2 ☆
The Conflict at the Center:
Skepticism and Rationality

SKEPTICAL EPISTEMOLOGY AND TACIT KNOWLEDGE

As John Gray (1986) has pointed out, Hayek's
epistemology has remained consistent throughout his
scholarly career. The key work for understanding his
epistemological position, The Sensory Order (1952),
also serves as an indispensable source for perceiving
the consistent underlying themes of his political
theory. Hayek's epistemological position is best
summarized by a proposition which he repeatedly
emphasizes in his work. The self-evident proposition
about human reason and knowledge is what Hayek refers
to as the constitutional limitation of the human mind,
or the primacy of tacit knowledge over theoretical
knowledge. The basis for this claim is laid in The
Sensory Order, where he distinguishes between two
"orders," the sensory (or the world as it is perceived
by human beings) and the physical (the world as it is
expressed via mathematical statements of relations
between objects). The sensory order is the one with
which people work in their daily lives; therefore
social scientists, interested in intelligible social
interactions, must contend with the perceived, sensory
order. This order is one of interpretation: perception
involves placing objects and events into classes. In
order for people to answer the question, "what is X?"
they bring into play a set of interpretations based on
learning and experience. This set of interpretations
constitutes tacit knowledge. People define "X" by
applying tacit knowledge, rules for evaluating a thing
in terms of relations between it and other objects or
subjects.
     According to Hayek, the intrinsic relationship
between tacit knowledge and the sensory order leads us
to conclude that the human mind is an "apparatus of
classification" which "can never fully explain its own

operations" (1952, p. 185). The mind itself is a
socially and culturally constituted product, unable to
divorce itself from the rules which allow the mind to
classify; the constituting rules of the mind always
remain beyond the understanding of the mind itself.
Within the realm of events which human beings can
understand, important limitations also exist. In a
remarkable passage, Hayek outlines the implicit nature
of the mind's operations, the vast number and
complexity of those operations, and the dynamic nature
of the process in which the mind constantly readjusts
its operations.

> The order of the sensory qualities is difficult to
> describe, not only because we are not explicitly
> aware of the relations between the different
> qualities but merely manifest these relations in
> the discriminations which we perform, and because
> the number and complexity of these relations is
> probably greater than anything which we could ever
> explicitly state or exhaustively describe, but
> also because...it is not a stable but a variable
> order (1952, p. 19).

Details of the world as perceived by the mind remain
forever beyond our reach; the best we can hope for is
knowledge of general characteristics.
      Hayek maintains that the nature of the mind and
sensory perception tells us there is no independent
"reality" which we can hope to see and describe clearly
one day. Because the mind is itself an order of events
or complex of relations (1952, p. 34), we are only and
always answering the question "what is X?" in terms of
X's relationship to other elements within a given
order. For social scientists to understand human
perceptions and actions, they must hope to understand
which role in what perceived order an action assumes.
      Every individual's perceived order is intricately
related to tacit knowledge, a store of inarticulate
knowledge that provides an instantly accessible guide
to behavior in a wide variety of situations. This
knowledge is supplied independently of reason through
learning and experience interpreted, initially, through
cultural traditions passed on by institutions such as
the family.
      If individuals often act upon inarticulate tacit
knowledge, human action is to be understood largely by
seeking regularities in classificatory responses.
Human reason as well as scientific theory can engage in
reconstructing and thereby articulating certain
portions of this knowledge, but the vast majority of it
will remain unarticulated. This implies that human
beings employ reason in responding to their environment

far less often than we might suppose. The roots of conscious knowledge in tacit knowledge initially shaped by cultural traditions <u>require</u>, in Hayek's view, that we examine traditions with care and respect.

Traditions do not determine the content of tacit knowledge, however, for tacit knowledge possessed by individuals is a highly personal kind of knowledge. It reflects one person's situation as that person perceives it, a reflection which according to Hayek's scheme remains unique and communicable to only a limited degree. That one person's tacit knowledge <u>can</u> be communicated to another is due to the fact that, as Hayek sees it, a common thread runs throughout individual stores of tacit knowledge. Tacit knowledge is first and foremost practical knowledge, knowledge about what "ensures the continued existence of the organism" (1952, p. 82). Here the full meaning of Hayek's relational answer to the question "What is X?" appears. Tacit knowledge is indeed always practical knowledge because in his interpretation it is tied to, and shaped by, perceptions of how responses to events will affect survival. The implication of this approach is that the enormous core of what we do as individuals is related to largely habitual perceptions about survival.

The Purpose of Life

The focus on survival and reproduction extends to Hayek's concept of human purpose. In <u>The Sensory Order</u>, Hayek states that what is meant by human "purposiveness" is "in the last instance really the same question as that of what ensures the continued existence of the organism" (1952, p. 8). This understanding of human purposiveness is echoed in one of Hayek's most recent lectures, "Our Moral Heritage" (<u>Knowledge, Evolution and Society,</u> 1983).

> Our morals, the morals which have prevailed, the morals of private property and honesty, are simply those which favour the practices that assist the multiplication of mankind.
> The economic calculus is a calculus of life: it guides us to do the sort of things that secure the most rapid increase in mankind. In a sense, I am prepared to defend this contention by saying that life has no other purpose than itself, by which I mean that we have been so adjusted that our actions contribute to produce more human beings than there existed before. But I do not think that there is any reason to be horrified by this (1983, pp. 50-51).

Despite Hayek's allusions to the wisdom contained in traditional stores of knowledge, it is clear that he does not view wisdom as a set of answers to the question, "what am I to do with my life?" For the wisdom to which he refers is "practical" knowledge, knowledge pertaining to the reproduction of life itself.

This view of wisdom and the position that "life has no other purpose than itself" is a consequence of the <u>limits</u> of human knowledge found in his epistemology, and informs his understanding of the self. The concept of the self with which he works is what Sandel (1982) terms the "unencumbered self." This self is unencumbered by any <u>constituting</u> aims and attachments; instead, "the values and relations we have are the products of choice, the possessions of a self given prior to its ends" (Sandel 1984, p. 169). The concept of agency for Hayek's version of the unencumbered self emerges as limited in two significant ways. First, purposiveness is related only to survival, rather than to a deepening understanding of a meaningful life or individual aspirations. Second, the unencumbered, choosing self is not often an autonomous, rational decision maker, because in Hayek's account that self generally simply <u>applies</u> tacit knowledge in a routine, habitual fashion. Hayek's understanding of the nature of human agency diverges, then, from classical rationalist views of individual agency, in ways which have serious consequences for his understanding of individual liberty.

Other Consequences of Hayek's Skepticism

One of Hayek's most compelling themes is that our theoretical knowledge will always be dwarfed by our tacit, unarticulated knowledge. Several consequences follow from this skeptical evaluation of the human capacity for theoretical knowledge. The first and most significant consequence is Hayek's defense of the market order as a coordinating mechanism in epistemological terms. The decentralized market, theoretically at least, allows individuals to draw upon their own particular store of tacit knowledge. This means that "that utilization of dispersed knowledge is achieved on which the well-being of the Great Society rests" (1976, p. 94). As Samuel Brittan puts it, "Hayek has stressed that markets are means of disseminating information diffused among millions of human beings....The market system is a 'discovery technique' rather than a way of allocating known resources among known wants with known techniques" (1983, p. 59).

Two other consequences of Hayek's skepticism have been discussed: his skeptical basis leads him into a philosophical pragmatism (McClain 1979, Gray 1980), and/or a moral skepticism bordering on ethical relativism (Acton 1961, Diamond 1980, McClain 1979). In both cases, critics charge, Hayek is led to an untenable position where he must defend the status quo. This defense, furthermore, must rest upon something other than moral principles.

Gray states the case most clearly. Hayek's epistemology is hard to distinguish from a "form of pragmatism with deeply skeptical implications....Those ways of thought which survive a natural selection process of competition with others are presumed to contain some truth about the world" (Gray 1980, p. 121). There appears, Stephen McClain contends, to be no test for what is good or bad other than persistence through time. Are there no absolute principles or reason or morality which transcend cultural evolution? Hayek's answer is, simply, "no."

> There can...be no <u>absolute</u> system of morals independent of the kind of social order in which a person lives, and the obligation incumbent upon us, to follow certain rules derives from the benefits we owe to the order in which we live (1976, pp. 26-27, emphasis added).

The assumption McClain, Arthur Diamond, and Gray all make is that Hayek's philosophical skepticism must be translated into a similarly radical skepticism in his political theory. In fact, Hayek maintains positions similar to those of Hume,[1] who has been described as both a philosophical skeptic and a "practical skeptic" (Marshall 1954). As a philosophical skeptic, Hume contends that no absolute principles can be proven to be "certainly true." As a practical skeptic, Hume counsels wariness before prescriptions claiming insight into absolute principles or rights. In everyday life, people reason necessarily from the incomplete evidence of experience without supposing they know the "truth" for all time (Marshall 1954, p. 251).

Hayek, it seems to me, makes a similar distinction. We cannot prove absolute principles because we can never have complete knowledge. We cannot prove that any values are immutable and eternal (1979, p. 166). Human reason is limited. To say that reason is limited, however, is not to say that it is useless. A liberal, Hayek contends, distrusts reason, "aware that we do not know all the answers and that he is not sure that the answers he has are certainly the right ones or even that we can find all the answers"

(1960, p. 406). The limits of reason and the impossibility of full knowledge are asserted in order to encourage an attitude of humility and reverence. The "heady wine of reason," says Hayek, "must be paired with modesty" (1967, p. 130). Thus we can reason about what past experience has shown to us, and suggest amendments to tried principles. But no one individual can have knowledge of an abstract set of principles which is good or true for mankind, because none of us can obtain an "independent" perspective on our cultural heritage. Our critiques can never be of the whole we see around us, but must be an examination of strands within the whole.

> No single human intelligence is capable of inventing the most appropriate abstract rules because those rules which have evolved in the process of growth of society embody the experience of many more trials and errors than any individual mind could acquire (1967, p. 88).

Hayek appears at this point to appeal to a rational analysis of experience rather than to an abstract scheme of rights or principles. Philosophically, we can never know with certainty what absolute values are "true." Practically, our reason is limited and shaped by experience. Within those limits, says Hayek, and provided we recognize them, lessons can be drawn from human experience about how to preserve and shape a free society.

HAYEK'S CRITIQUE OF CONSTRUCTIVIST RATIONALISM

What are the lessons from experience we can draw, and what are we to do with such information? Here we encounter in heightened form the controversy relating to the appropriateness of proposing constitutional reform against a background of lauding cultural evolution and stressing the limits of human knowledge. Two separate issues must be identified at the outset of this discussion. The first is whether or not Hayek's attack on constructivist rationalism has the consequence that any suggestions for the preservation of a free society become an inconsistent if not contradictory project. I will argue in this chapter that certain kinds of suggestions for change or reform are _not_ inconsistent with Hayek's attack on constructivist rationalism. The second issue which arises is whether his discussion of ordered liberty, including as it does a case for the necessity of reliance upon culturally evolved products, provides any guidelines for ascertaining when appropriately designed reforms (not constructivist rationalist types) may be undertaken. This issue will be addressed in subsequent chapters.

What is the central argument against constructivist rationalism made by Hayek? Both Gray (1986) and Calvin Hoy (1984) identify the main argument in terms of Hayek's opposition to what he calls the "fatal conceit." This conceit is that the social order is the result of some intelligent design. Usually this stems from what Gray calls the error of believing that "the order we discover--in nature, in our minds and in society--has been put there by some designing mind" (1986, p. 30). This leads to the belief, as Hoy puts it, "in a human creator for society, language, and law...[and the resulting position] that as these institutions have been humanly created they can be refashioned or completely changed by human beings following a rational design for human life" (1984, p. 6). In Hayek's own words, constructivist rationalism rests on the "conception which assumes that all social institutions are, and ought to be, the product of deliberate design" (1973, p. 5). Human reason is regarded not only as sufficient to construct social institutions but also to completely remodel an entire society. Because human reason can obtain conscious knowledge of cause and effect relationships, constructivist rationalists assume reason is powerful enough to achieve control over the destiny of humanity.

Hayek denies that reason can obtain such knowledge and argues that "the desire to use our reason to turn the whole of society into one rationally directed engine" (1973, p. 32) fails to recognize the role which spontaneous evolutionary processes play in free civilizations. This limited assessment of the powers of human reason appears to offer the basis for what I view as misinterpretations of Hayek's attack upon constructivist rationalism. Barry, for example, notes Hayek's concern over the "rise of a 'constructivist' outlook which, in the attempt to design institutions with specific purposes, obliterate all the advantages of spontaneous action." He goes on to say that Hayek believes that "reason is an inadequate instrument for the construction and appraisal of institutions" (1984, p. 280).

Yet when we look at Hayek's specific description of constructivist rationalism, it is not the design, construction, or appraisal of particular institutions which he condemns, but the desire to recreate human society as a whole in a new mold, a desire which almost inevitably involves the use of centralized coercive direction. In <u>Road to Serfdom</u>, Hayek says that liberal (or "true") individualism, which provides guidelines for deliberately creating a system in which competition will work beneficially, "is the exact opposite of that intellectual hubris which is at the root of the demand for <u>comprehensive</u> direction of the social process" (1944, p. 166). The hubris of constructivist rationalism involves the idea of "making the social order <u>wholly</u> dependent on design" (1973, p. 5). The "basic order" of society cannot rest <u>entirely</u> on design; constructivist rationalism as a conception is flawed because of a "misconception of the forces which have made the Great Society and civilization possible" (1973, p. 6).

The key distinction should be regarded as that between "shaping" and "directing," or planning. In general, Hayek labels all modern planners "constructivist rationalists," individuals who flirt with hubris because of their inflated concept of the creative potential of human reason. It is their failure to respect the accomplishments of spontaneously ordered individual actions that draws Hayek's passionate denunciation.

> The dispute between the modern planners and their opponents is, therefore, <u>not</u> a dispute on whether we ought to choose intelligently between the various possible organizations of society;...It is a dispute about what is the best way of employing foresight and systematic thinking in planning our common affairs. The question is whether for this purpose it is better that the holder of coercive power should confine himself in general to creating conditions under which the knowledge and initiative of individuals are given the best scope so that <u>they</u> can plan most successfully; or whether a rational utilization of our resources requires <u>central</u> direction and organization of all our activities according to some consciously constructed "blueprint" (1978, p. 234).

This appears to be the understanding of constructivist rationalism that Gray perceives Hayek to denounce. Gray notes that Hayek's views entail "that the object of public policy should be confined to the design or reform of institutions within which unknown individuals make and execute their own, largely unpredictable plans of life" (1986, p. 80). He adds that while we give up the notion of "consciously controlling" social life, we continue to hope for "<u>cultivating</u> the general conditions in which beneficial results may be expected to emerge" (1986, p. 81).

Recognizing the implicit approval of efforts toward cultivation embedded in Hayek's attack on constructivist rationalism draws our attention to a number of subtle parts to his critique which have been

overlooked.   This lack of attention may be due to the
fragmented nature of these parts, which I will attempt
to draw together into a coherent theme.   The theme
embedded in his critique of constructivist rationalism
is the necessity for exercise of the faculty of
judgement if liberal societies are to survive and
flourish.
    My attention to a theme of judgement appears,
initially, ill-placed.   Both Barry (1984) and Gray
(1986), in their explorations of the meaning of tacit
knowledge in Hayek's work, note the absence of any
discussion of judgement in Hayek's treatment of tacit
knowledge.   Barry in fact contends that Hayek has
developed a view of human behavior as almost
exclusively rule-governed, "offering an explanation of
rule-following as almost automatic and necessarily
unreflective, which seems somewhat at odds with the
classical liberal idea of individual rationality"
(1984, p. 281).   Gray notes that Hayek diverges from
Kant on the matter of judgement.   For Kant, "knowledge
requires judgement, a special faculty, the
Urteilskraft...In the sense that we must exercise this
faculty of judgement even before we can apply a rule,
it is action which is at the root of our very knowledge
itself" (1986, p. 14).   Gray argues that Hayek is not
concerned "with this ultimate dependency of rule
following upon judgement" (1986, p. 14).
    I argue that Hayek attempts to avoid the notion of
judgement but ultimately relies upon it in spite of his
preference for avoiding it.   I believe that the
crucial distinction between "critical" and
"constructivist" rationalists is that the former
exercise judgement, while the latter do not.   Jon
Elster's definition of judgement helps to clarify my
claim.   Judgement is "the capacity to synthesize vast
and diffuse information that more or less clearly bears
on the problem at hand, in such a way that no element
or set of elements is given undue importance" (1983, p.
16).   Constructivist rationalists attribute vastly
more importance to the expertise of human reason than
Hayek claims they should.
    Hayek tells us that adherents of constructivist
rationalism fail to understand the necessity for
submission required to engage in genuine learning as
well as to approach the knowledge of the most
appropriate use of human rationality (1979).   If
individuals are to become rational, they must "submit
to general principles" (1960, p. 179), recognizing that
"all generalizations we can formulate rest on higher
generalizations which we don't know...we try to
discover them, but it is an unending process" (1960, p.
209).   In the same way as the mind is governed by rules
we can never completely know, so is reason guided by

social forces we cannot fully identify. What is
required is an "attitude of humility before this social
process and of tolerance to other opinions" (1944, p.
166).

Critical rationalists, in contrast to
constructivist rationalists, are able to see reason
situated within the matrix provided by social processes
and tacit knowledge, preventing an overestimation of
the powers of human reason. Recognition of the circumscribed role of reason, attained through acceptance of
the social processes that permit the growth of reason,
is far more likely to issue in judgements valuing
cultural traditions and making their preservation a
high priority. If judgement is to play such an
important role in preserving fundamental traditions of
a free society, why is the subject not directly
addressed? A similar question arises with Hayek's
discussion of the value of tacit knowledge. Why didn't
Hayek pay more attention to the role of judgement in
the application of tacit knowledge? For clearly a bulk
of tacit knowledge may supply several routes of action,
and possibly conflicting ones. Individuals select from
tacit knowledge in some form.

I believe that Hayek's avoidance of this topic
reflects his inability to envision the self in terms
other than those of the unencumbered self. For the
self capable of making judgements and reflecting upon
choices (including those indicated by tacit knowledge)
resembles the situated self more than the unencumbered
self. Hayek is uncomfortable with the concept of the
situated self because the situated self is
"constituted" in part by conceptions of the good that
are not created solely by that individual. To talk
about the situated self in this way implies that there
are commonly held and believed theories of the good
relevant to the political and economic matters Hayek
discusses. In other words, once we introduce notions
of judgement, it seems difficult to avoid the ideas of
"good" and "bad" choices reflecting a set of
fundamental values.

As a liberal, Hayek is reluctant to set out a
theory of the good. He has no desire to impose a view
of what is "right for man" on others. Thus he
comments, "it's not the task of political philosophy to
prescribe to the individual the ideals he ought to
hold" (1975, p. 11). Despite this disclaimer, Hayek
does rely upon a theory of the good. He appears to fit
the "recurrent pattern" William Galston identifies in
contemporary liberalism. "Each of these contemporary
liberal theories begins by promising to do without a
substantive theory of the good; each ends by betraying
that promise" (1982, p. 625). Hayek's reliance, like
that of the theorists Galston discusses, is covert.

There are two indicators of the presence of covert reliance on a theory of the good. One is the quest Hayek follows throughout his work, and announces in The Constitution of Liberty (1960), to reclaim a liberal utopian vision able to compete with socialism in capturing the imagination of the people. Not only does this statement of purpose imply that Hayek will work within a theory of the good, but also that for individuals to support liberalism, they must be acquainted with a liberal theory of the good. The second indicator is the often implicit and occasionally explicit glorification of human learning, which I believe is the central element of his theory of the good. The development of one's ability to learn to the fullest is defined by Hayek to be good. In using the gift of intelligence, and expanding knowledge, man creates good for himself and the rest of society. We may not become happier or better able to control our world, but this, says Hayek, does not matter. "What matters is the process of learning: in it man enjoys the gift of his intelligence" (1960, p. 41). Use of intelligence to advance knowledge is made possible rather than prevented by recognition of the knowledge contained in existing institutions. But this recognition rests upon human judgement of the value and importance of such knowledge.

As a classical liberal, however, Hayek is also committed to the principle that the ends of the individual, whatever these may be, are to be supreme. Accordingly, he relies primarily on a "formal" justification of the liberal state, in which such a state is desirable "not because it promotes a specific way of life, but precisely because it alone does not do so" (Galston 1982, p. 621). The covert theory of the good which I have outlined reveals a commitment to individuals as social beings, for whom individual ends are related to social ends. Hayek does sometimes speak of individuals as social creatures "whose whole nature and character is determined by their existence in society" (1948, p. 6). But he does not pursue the implications of his theory of the good for his concept of the self or human agency, with unfortunate effects for his philosophy's overall coherence. His call for favorable judgements of tacit knowledge and cultural tradition strikes a discordant note. Had he brought his theory of the good to the front and center of his work, that call would seem more appropriate and far more comprehensible.

CRITICAL RATIONALITY

With the background established above, we can now

turn to Hayek's understanding and application of critical rationality. His view of critical rationality can be summarized in two statements. One is that "we must shed the illusion that we can deliberately 'create the future of mankind'" (1979, p. 152). A second is that "[g]overnment is of necessity the product of intellectual design" (1979, p. 152). Once we have given up the notion of complete control over the future, it becomes possible to seek to learn what elements in our existence we can control. Thus Hayek believes we can profit by studying how earlier attempts to design government have turned out. There is, he asserts, "much we ought to have learned from the history of the last two hundred years" (1973, p. 2) which the founders of liberal constitutionalism, even with all their wisdom, could not have known. Intellectual design of government is necessary if principles gleaned from experience are to be applied. In the discussion that follows, I illustrate Hayek's understanding of critical rationality by exploring his constitutional design.

Hayek's constitution results from his critique of modern democracies. He focuses on the structure of an interest-group democracy, the type of democracy found in the United States and Western Europe. That structure jeopardizes liberty in two ways: by direct interference in individual lives and by corrupting the law binding individuals into a polity. This critique directly challenges the pluralist paradigm of demo-cratic politics. According to this paradigm, the clash of interest groups in the public arena constitutes a legitimate, working form of democracy. Hayek maintains that the end result of interest-group democracy does not constitute "majority rule" and eventually leads to a breakdown in both effective and legitimate government.

The strong moral sense of Hayek's attack reflects his belief that representative democracy as we know it is corrupt and unjust. Leaders in democratic governments are "forced to bring together and keep together a majority by satisfying the demands of a multitude of special interests, each of which will consent to the special benefits granted to other groups only at the price of their own special interests being equally considered" (1979, p. 99). Any concept of a public interest or public good vanishes as "pork-barrel politics" dominates. Leaders in such governments cannot assure the rule of law, which aims at "the abolition of all privilege, be it in favor of the strong or the weak" (1955, p. 48).

Hayek's account of the causes of this corruption of the rule of law identifies several interacting factors. These include institutional/structural

factors, the power of ideas, and evolving cultural
attitudes. Of the three, he tends to focus most
directly on the structural failure of democratic
republics to successfully limit governmental power
outlined above. This failure, he appears to believe,
is largely a result of unsuccessful constitutional
design. The logical endpoint of this focus is on
constitutional remedies. Yet in Hayek's account,
structural factors alone do not explain the problems of
interest-group democracies. He also argues that a
complex set of modern ideas and cultural attitudes has
led to increased corruption.

The prime candidate for the most devastating idea
according to Hayek is the rise of the notion of "social
justice." Social justice, or the demand to place
people into more equal material positions, has partly
resulted from, and in turn increased the demand for
constructivist rationalism. It also served to
legitimate the transition from the principle of equal
treatment under the law to arbitrariness (1979, p.
103). The attractiveness of social justice has led
people and legislators alike to justify a wide variety
of measures directly benefiting certain sets of people.
The granting of benefits through legislation, combined
with the mechanics of attaining majority coalitions has
had a deadly escalating effect.

> Dispensing gratuities at the expense of somebody
> else who cannot be readily identified became the
> most attractive way of buying majority support.
> But a parliament or government which becomes a
> charitable institution thereby becomes exposed to
> irresistible blackmail. And it soon ceases to be
> the "deserts" but becomes exclusively the
> "political necessity" which determines which
> groups are to be favored at general expense (1979,
> p. 103).

A third cause of the corruption of democratic
structures Hayek identifies is a changing attitude
toward the market. Hayek points to a change in values
brought about by the increasing number of individuals
who work in large organizations. Communities in which
entrepreneurs are outnumbered by employees of
organizations may contain few individuals who
understand how "the market" works.

> Such communities will not ascribe the different
> fortunes of its members to the operation of an
> impersonal mechanism which serves to guide the
> direction of efforts, but to some human power that
> ought to allocate shares according to merit (1976,
> p. 81).

The crucial factor appears to be that a livelihood for individuals in organizations depends less on following abstract price signals than in operating "within a small group joining for a common purpose" (1979a, p. 6). The rules on which the market rests, Hayek suggests, become less relevant for many people because of this insulation from the market.

There are some implications of this line of analysis which Hayek has not pursued but that point to grave problems in the perpetuation of the rules and, perhaps, the values on which a market order rests. Does the market order require that people understand how the abstract price-system works? The answers Hayek gives are confusing. Occasionally he seems to think that as long as the Western civilized tradition containing the basic cultural rules on which the development of the market has rested is maintained, the market order will persist. Thus one goal of his work is to keep that tradition alive. This answer to the question is consistent with the position that the purposes rules serve are often not fully understood by the rule-followers and need not be so understood.

If, however, such traditions are destroyed by spontaneous institutional growth within the market itself (such as the growth of more and larger organizations), then the need for rational understanding of the market as a system is more pressing. Hayek is <u>not</u> optimistic about the possibility that such a widespread understanding will develop. If the preservation of the market order requires that "the people rationally understand that certain rules are indispensable to preserve the social division of labor, it may well be doomed" (1979, p. 206, n. 54). Those who <u>could</u> teach the public, Hayek gloomily acknowledges, the intellectuals, are unlikely to do so. Samuel Brittan echoes Hayek's pessimism when he comments that the "very existence of this self-regulating [market] system is quite unsuspected by ninety-nine per cent of the population" (1983, p. 59).

If a change in ideas and attitudes is due in large part to the changing nature of people's experiences, then will constitutional rules have much effect in preventing abuses of liberty which occur with market interference? And at a more fundamental level, how can we know what effects are likely to be generated by institutional reform, given our limitations of knowledge? These questions raise the issue of the relationship between institutions and ideas. Hayek does tell us, generally, that institutions affect ideas, and vice versa. How would his specific design affect the ideas he identifies as dangers for Western civilization? These topics are not explored in any depth. Hayek maintains that it is useful to explore

factors, the power of ideas, and evolving cultural
attitudes. Of the three, he tends to focus most
directly on the structural failure of democratic
republics to successfully limit governmental power
outlined above. This failure, he appears to believe,
is largely a result of unsuccessful constitutional
design. The logical endpoint of this focus is on
constitutional remedies. Yet in Hayek's account,
structural factors alone do not explain the problems of
interest-group democracies. He also argues that a
complex set of modern ideas and cultural attitudes has
led to increased corruption.

The prime candidate for the most devastating idea
according to Hayek is the rise of the notion of "social
justice." Social justice, or the demand to place
people into more equal material positions, has partly
resulted from, and in turn increased the demand for
constructivist rationalism. It also served to
legitimate the transition from the principle of equal
treatment under the law to arbitrariness (1979, p.
103). The attractiveness of social justice has led
people and legislators alike to justify a wide variety
of measures directly benefiting certain sets of people.
The granting of benefits through legislation, combined
with the mechanics of attaining majority coalitions has
had a deadly escalating effect.

> Dispensing gratuities at the expense of somebody
> else who cannot be readily identified became the
> most attractive way of buying majority support.
> But a parliament or government which becomes a
> charitable institution thereby becomes exposed to
> irresistible blackmail. And it soon ceases to be
> the "deserts" but becomes exclusively the
> "political necessity" which determines which
> groups are to be favored at general expense (1979,
> p. 103).

A third cause of the corruption of democratic
structures Hayek identifies is a changing attitude
toward the market. Hayek points to a change in values
brought about by the increasing number of individuals
who work in large organizations. Communities in which
entrepreneurs are outnumbered by employees of
organizations may contain few individuals who
understand how "the market" works.

> Such communities will not ascribe the different
> fortunes of its members to the operation of an
> impersonal mechanism which serves to guide the
> direction of efforts, but to some human power that
> ought to allocate shares according to merit (1976,
> p. 81).

Establishing and maintaining distinct representative bodies to carry out governmental functions can be facilitated by the separation of powers--a particular kind of constitutional device once central to the liberal tradition because it was believed to create limited government. As a critical rationalist, Hayek seeks to understand the value of this tradition and apply it to contemporary times. He relies upon recent works by William Gwyn (1965) and Maurice Vile (1967) to supplement his own perceptions of this tradition. As a result, he identifies two core elements of the concept of the separation of powers: an analysis of governmental powers in terms of functions and the belief that the ideal of liberty can be realized through the implementation of a separation of powers (Gwyn 1965). Hayek draws primarily upon the functional analysis which recognized a distinction between nomothetical and gubernative functions (Gwyn 1965, p. 31). These early distinctions were less concerned with balancing or checking branches of government and more concerned with effectively separating rule making from the enforcement of such rules. Hayek sees himself recovering this early concept of a separation of powers and applying it in his constitutional design.

In his application, however, he adjusts the traditional approach by applying it to what he sees as the primary functions of modern government, rule making and the supply of certain services to the population. The first function of government is to preserve order by the identification and enforcement of rules of just conduct. This function is justified in Hayek's thought by a characteristically liberal view of the nature of man. "[A]ll men in the pursuit of immediate aims are apt--or, because of the limitation of their intellect, in fact bound--to violate rules of conduct which they would nevertheless wish to see generally observed" (1960, p. 179). When a government is not strong enough to fulfill this function, anarchy results.

The second function of government Hayek identifies, one quite distinct from the first, is to supply certain services to the population. Hayek here accepts the possibility of more than the "minimal state," reflecting the emphasis on government as a legitimate agent for the production of certain public goods established early in his work. Such a state requires a set of rules for the direction of government supply of services. Hayek clearly believes both of these functions are compatible with individual liberty.

He suggests that the Founding Fathers hoped to limit government and protect freedom by a separation of powers between branches of government. Their scheme failed to accomplish their goals. The reason for their failure was that the functions of law making on the one side, and law-administration as well as direction of the government on the other, were not distinguished. In other words, the same representative assemblies were charged with laying down rules of individual conduct and laying down rules concerning the organization and conduct of government (1967, p. 169).[2] His constitutional design, Hayek contends, "would for the first time make possible that real separation of powers which has never yet existed" (1978, p. 96). He categorically rejects any notion that a separation of powers exists in either Great Britain or the United States. "[T]he two paradigms of democratic government...are really two monstrosities and caricatures of the ideal of separation of powers" (1979, p. 179, n. 10).

The Constitutional Model

The fullest exposition of the details of his constitutional model is in The Political Order of a Free People (1979, pp. 105-127). Hayek's proposal contains three parts, all of which are designed to maintain the distinction between governmental functions he sees as central to the idea of a separation of powers. The first part consists of the "Basic Clause" of the Constitution; the second is the Constitutional Court; and the third is the legislative branch consisting of the Legislative and Governmental Assemblies.

The Basic Clause. The Basic Clause is intended to do two things: to define the limits of the coercive power of the state, and to specify the organizational structure of the state. In the latter capacity, the Basic Clause must reflect decisions about the state as a service provider. In the former, it reflects ideas about the proper role(s) of government in providing for individual liberty. Hayek does not emphasize either the interrelatedness of these two aspects or the extent to which acceptance of them must rest on a community commitment to general principles. He is content to describe the constitution as a "protective superstructure designed to regulate the continuous process of developing an existing body of law" (1979, p. 122). It is to accomplish this regulation "only by stating the general attributes such laws must possess in order to entitle government to use coercion for their enforcement" (1979, p. 122).

As a "protective superstructure," however, the constitution represents not an empty framework but in fact a set of political ideals. As Hayek surely knows, the idea of a constitution from classical times to the present involves <u>both</u> moral goals of a community and a set of legal rules for governmental organizations (for discussion, see Spencer 1978, Mulgan 1977). Acceptance of Hayek's Basic Clause in fact commits one to his version of the basic principles of ordered liberty. He does not discuss the degree to which some kind of attachment to or reverence for a constitution is required, despite his own focus on the importance of tradition.

Hayek's reluctance to discuss the Basic Clause as a set of political ideals is a direct reflection of his preference for formally justifying the state and avoiding the idea of judgement. He prefers to avoid thinking of a constitution as an embodiment of political ideals. Such a view has two consequences, neither of which Hayek is keen about. First, it means that a government "embodies a more-than-minimal conception of the good" (Galston 1982, p. 627). Operating with a covert theory of the good, Hayek cannot directly acknowledge this consequence without reconsidering his defense of the neutral state. Second, when a constitution is seen to embody political ideals, then constitutional debate becomes highly political. This consequence presents Hayek with another set of difficulties relating to his view of "the political."

His view of the political reveals the full extent of his dependence upon the model of the unencumbered self. For such an individual, politics is related only to external matters of material advantage. Hayek's reliance upon this view of the meaning of politics for the self is shown in his views about the "dethronement of politics." While implicitly acknowledging the critical role of politics in liberal societies by presenting a constitutional design, Hayek offers a design that he hopes will lead to the "dethronement of politics" (1979, p. 128). The basic questions of the role of government, it appears, are to be solved, once and for all, at the constitutional level. While Hayek admits that defects might be discovered requiring amendment, he fails to discuss an appropriate amending procedure (1979, p. 123). He leaves no room for basic questions about legitimate state action to appear on the political agenda.

The broader implication is that Hayek does not envision political struggle including debate about exactly what certain traditions mean and what consequences they carry for current times. The perception that the attainment of agreement on the meaning of such traditions is one of the ongoing processes of democratic politics is absent; it is far from clear that Hayek is willing to trust the outcomes of democratically-produced adaptations to tradition.

Politics in Hayek's constitutional democracy remains a politics of bargaining, a politics congenial to the vision of the unencumbered self. Hayek does not wish to change the substantive nature of democratic politics; he simply wants to change the rules of the bargaining process. Examination of the other parts of his proposal supports the view that a politics of bargaining about comparative advantage is acceptable as long as that bargaining is constrained by firm limits.

The Constitutional Court. The second part of Hayek's constitutional design is the Constitutional Court. The limiting function of this court is clear. "Its decisions often would have to be...that nobody at all was entitled to take certain kinds of coercive measures" (1979, p. 121). Limits on governmental action are to be strictly enforced. This court is to decide disputes between legislative bodies, and, more importantly, to judge whether new laws conform to the specifications for just law set down in the constitution. A constitutional provision for such judgements is not particularly controversial, since it rests upon a long Western tradition of reliance upon such courts for adjudicating intra-governmental disputes. Hayek has not indicated how members of the court would initially be selected, although subsequent members would be chosen from retired members of the Legislative Assembly.

The Governmental Assembly. The third part of Hayek's proposal we will consider here is his suggestion that two distinct representative assemblies be elected. The Governmental Assembly would act much as do present representative assemblies in the United States and Great Britain, but would be restricted both by the rules of the constitution and the rules of just conduct approved by the Legislative Assembly. The Governmental Assembly could be run along party lines (and Hayek expects this assembly to elect the chief executive officer in a parliamentary manner). As indicated above, one enormous difference would be present: decisions on expenditures could not, theoretically, be accompanied by ingenuous schemes to either require someone else to finance the costs or disguise the burden imposed on the taxpayer (1979, p. 127).

The Legislative Assembly. The most interesting element of Hayek's proposal is the second representative body, the Legislative Assembly. Because of his somewhat muddled discussion of how these individuals would be elected, the proposal as it stands is sure to inspire charges of "aristocratic" sympathies. Yet I think Hayek's intention as to what purpose this body should serve is clear. The Legislative Assembly is to be elected differently than the Governmental Assembly.

Election by contemporaries is suggested.

> [I]t would seem wise...to ask each group of people
> of the same age once in their lives, say in the
> calendar year in which they reached the age of 45,
> to select from their midst representatives to
> serve for fifteen years (1979, p. 113).

Along with other institutional provisions, such a
method of election could produce an independent body of
individuals. What would be the consequence? This
system of election "would come nearer to producing that
ideal of the political theorists, a senate of wise and
honorable men, than any system yet tried" (1978, p.
96). Hayek quite deliberately links his proposal to an
ancient quest in political philosophy: how to assure
good and wise rule by men over men. The senate of his
plan, he believes, would respond to public opinion
rather than the will or interests of groups of
individuals.

The focus on opinion allows us to see that the
Legislative Assembly is the body in which debate about
the meaning of traditions is to take place. For
opinion, as Hayek uses the term, refers in fact to
traditional moral beliefs, what he considers to be
lasting and permanent dispositions about what kinds of
acts are right and wrong. The unreflective nature of
such moral "judgements" is made clear when he tells us
that opinions are held by individuals "without their
having any known reasons for them except that they are
the traditions of the society in which they have grown
up" (1978, p. 85). Legislation proper (rule making)
should be governed by traditional moral views about
what kinds of action are right and wrong. The tasks of
determining what those opinions are and how they should
be translated into law are to be entrusted to
legislators selected for their probity, wisdom, and
judgement (1979, p. 112). Debates in the chambers of
the Legislative Assembly allow a select few to make
judgements about political ideals.

The Governmental Assembly, and politics in
general, will then be appropriately restrained. For
everyday politics can be regarded as matters of
conflict over "will" rather than "opinion." Hayek
explicitly contrasts opinion and will, arguing that
"will always refers to particular actions serving
particular ends, and the will ceases when the action is
taken and the end (terminus) reached" (1978, p. 85).
Current democratic institutions facilitate the will of
numerous groups without serving the opinion of the
majority. Majority rule does not in fact occur,
following this line of analysis; it cannot, Hayek
maintains, given the current structure of the American

and British democratic republics.

Hayek has reopened a discussion about how a free
republic must be constituted if traditional morals, or
majority opinion is to be translated into law which
retains some claim to represent common conceptions of
the good. The covert theory of the good with which
Hayek operates is present in his constitutional
proposals. Hayek the liberal seeks a way to guarantee
the preservation of the traditional beliefs which have
made liberalism viable. He seeks, ultimately,
acceptable "nonliberal" bulwarks for the liberal state.

PARALLELS TO MADISONIAN THOUGHT

The extent to which Hayek's constitutional
thought, and the solution it represents for shoring up
the liberal polity, is compatible with the concept of
the unencumbered self can be examined by comparing his
work with that of James Madison. Madison's analysis of
the political situation in the American colonies
requiring constitutional remedy bears striking
resemblances to Hayek's analysis of a bargaining
democracy. The need for a form of government which
could uphold liberty as well as general opinions in the
presence of individuals pursuing their own interests
was demonstrated for Madison by the situation in the
colonies prior to the Constitutional Convention. For
example, he was disturbed by indications that
particular interests were prevailing in state
assemblies. Members of these assemblies were
"everywhere observed to lose sight of the aggregate
interests of the Community, and even to sacrifice them
to the interests or prejudices of their respective
constituents" (1901, vol. V, p. 284). The pursuit of
particular interests could degenerate rapidly into
licentious greed.

> But the mild voice of reason, pleading the cause
> of an enlarged and permanent interest, is but too
> often drowned before public bodies as well as
> individuals, by the clamor of an impatient avidity
> for immediate and immoderate gain (1961, p. 268).

Greed had a place in human affairs--in commerce; but it
became a dangerous force in politics.

Greed became particularly dangerous in the guise
of impatient popular interest-based demands placed upon
the national government. The idea of time for
independent deliberation occupied Madison. Madison's
structuring of the government so as to "filter" popular
demands and to defend people against "their own
temporary errors and delusions" (1961, p. 384) owed

much to Hume's conception of government as a filtering device inducing people "to transform their short-term perceptions of their private interests into long-term understanding of the general identity of interests--and, in that sense, of the public good" (Pocock 1975, p. 495).

This filtering supplied one part of Madison's solution to the problem of "virtuous" representation in the American republic. The Senate in Madison's plan, like the Legislative Assembly in Hayek's, was designed to provide a space for independent and presumably public-minded individuals. Madison also hoped to limit government, even government by thoughtful representatives. He intended, of course, not only a separation of functions, but also a set of checks between (jealous) branches of the government. The checks, he hoped, would preserve the separation of powers.

Madison had other, less well-known remedies for the problem of securing good representatives in a commercial republic. Madison relied upon American citizens to act as guardians of the liberty which enabled them to pursue their interests. If they did not have sufficient "virtue" even for this, he implied that there could be little hope for the republic. "To suppose that any form of government will secure liberty or happiness without _any_ virtue in the people, is a chimerical idea" (Padover 1953, p. 49, emphasis added). As long as some virtue, some concern beyond an individual's purely private affairs, existed, Madison believed the republic might endure. The key lay in the development of a reverential attachment to the Constitution as a kind of public property.

> The people who are authors of [constitutional liberty], must also be its guardians. Their eyes must be ever ready to mark, their voice to pronounce, and their arm to repel or repair aggressions on the authority of their constitutions; the highest authority next to their own, because the immediate work of their own, and the most sacred part of their property, as recognizing and recording the title to every other (1901, vol. VI, p. 93).

Like Hayek, Madison believed that traditional maxims of conduct found in established opinions had a vital role to play. He was concerned that "permanent and constitutional maxims of conduct [may] prevail over occasional impressions and inconsiderate pursuits" (1901, vol. VI, pp. 89-90). Madison never elucidated a list of such maxims--nor how these norms were to be established. He did imply what two of the maxims might

be, however.   One concerned taxation, and the other,
the nature of legislature law.   I will discuss each of
these in order to bring out how Hayek's constitutional
design embodies each of these rules in a way the
American Constitution did not.

On the matter of taxation, Madison demonstrates an
appreciation for the subtleties and important
consequences of different forms of taxation.   In the
passage from which I quote, Madison is pondering how to
prevent declaration of war based on popular sentiment.

> Each generation should be made to bear the burden
> of its own wars, instead of carrying them on, at
> the expense of other generations...each generation
> should not only bear its own burdens, but...the
> taxes composing them, should include a due
> proportion of such as by their direct operation
> keep the people awake, along with those, which
> being wrapped up in other payments, may leave them
> asleep, to misapplications of their money" (1901,
> vol. VI, p. 90).

Madison was not specific on the proper
characteristics of law.   In his critique of the "Vices
of the Political System of the United States," (1787),
Madison noted some problems in the law-making
situation.   He comments upon the evil of the
"multiplicity of laws" in various states.   It is
accompanied by a daily "mutability," which
"emphatically denotes a vicious legislation."   Finally,
such laws were unjust, bringing into question "the
fundamental principle of republican Government, that
the majority who rule in such governments are the
safest Guardians both of public Good and private
rights" (1901, vol. II, pp. 365-366).   How did Madison
propose to deal with such a situation?   While he did
not approach Hayek's division of legislative powers
(relying instead on public virtue), he did recognize
that different kinds of laws could usefully be
distinguished.

> The acts of political society may be divided into
> three classes: 1.   The fundamental constitution
> of the Government;   2.   Laws involving some
> stipulation which renders them irrevocable at the
> will of the Legislature;   3.   Laws involving no
> such irrevocable quality (1901, vol. V, p. 437).

Madison proposed, several times, that the national
legislature be given a "veto" over laws passed by the
states (Hobson 1979).   He hoped the majority at the
national level would be more disinterested, or
"independent" in Hayek's terms.

Hayek would maintain that Madison's separation of powers in fact did not correct the problems of taxation and law making he describes. The national legislature of the United States is only rarely thought of as a body of citizens dedicated to and honored for their pursuit of the public good. Yet the form of government Hayek critiques bears striking similarities to the kind of government Madison called an "impostor" of "venal spirit."

A government operating by corrupt influence; substituting the motive of private interest in place of public duty; converting its pecuniary dispensations into bounties to favorites, or bribes to opponents; accommodating its measures to the avidity of a part of the nation instead of the benefit of the whole (1901, vol. VI, p. 94).[3]

Madison believed the American experiment would provide the "government for which philosophy has been searching;" he hoped America's "glory" would be "completed by every improvement on the [republican] theory which experience may teach" (1901, vol. VI, p. 94). Hayek's design, like Madison's, remains firmly committed to a politics of bargaining, but one whose excesses are limited by constitutional improvement based on the teachings of experience.

NOTES

1.   This is the first of a number of references to similarities between Hayek and Hume; I have not explored the parallels in detail but suspect it is a topic worthy of further research.
2.   The distinction phrased in this way Hayek credits to Hume.
3.   In much the same manner, Burke contends that "to give a direction, a form, a technical dress, and a specific sanction, to the general sense of the community, is the true end of legislation" (1884, vol. II, p. 225).

☆ 3 ☆
The Unconstructed Civilization and the Need for Skepticism

In Hayek's discussion of ordered liberty, he argues in favor of positive evaluations of surviving cultural products such as traditions of behavior and social institutions. In this chapter I will identify as precisely as possible the nature of Hayek's defense of what I will term "unconstructed" institutions as products of cultural evolution. While I will attempt to specify what Hayek means to defend when he discusses the proper role of evolutionary forces in a free society, I am equally interested in exploring how he relates critical reason (on both the individual and societal scales) to the ongoing process of cultural evolution.

The relationship between critical reason and cultural evolution must be clarified if we are to be able to decide when we should venture into design rather than opting in favor of respect for surviving institutions. As I will show, the answer to this question remains unclear throughout Hayek's work, and if anything is eclipsed in his most recent writings about cultural evolution. For there, the role of reason appears to dwindle away at an alarming pace. Not only is all progress based upon tradition, and not only are most rules of behavior adopted without rational understanding, but in his account, "[t]radition is not something constant but the process of selection guided <u>not by reason</u> but by success." And, finally, our "social order depends on a system of views and opinions which we imbibe, inherit, and learn from a tradition <u>that we cannot modify</u>" (1983, p. 56, emphasis added).

The task of this chapter is to understand how Hayek arrived at this position. Against the powerful rationalist tradition, Hayek contends that he juxtaposes a more humble conception focusing on cultural evolution. His approach to the topic of

cultural or social evolution is complex--and made
confusing because both explanatory and normative
elements are involved in his treatment of the subject.
I will attempt to avoid a similar confusion in this
chapter by separating out the explanatory and normative
strands. I will look first at how Hayek came to
explain social order in an advanced society via an
evolutionary approach, and then assess the normative
implications he has drawn from this approach. It is in
the normative implications he identifies that his
initial humility seems to be transformed into a kind of
blind faith in the forces of evolution.

ORIGINS OF HAYEK'S VIEW OF CULTURAL EVOLUTION

Hayek has developed his understanding of cultural
evolution from two sources. One is the eighteenth-
century theory of individualism developed by David
Hume, Adam Smith, and Adam Ferguson. The central role
of the market as an evolved spontaneous order these
political economists emphasize was subsequently
reformulated by the Austrian economist, Carl Menger.
The second source Hayek acknowledges is the skeptical
conservatism of Edmund Burke.[1]
For Hayek, the eighteenth-century political
economists' analysis of the market alongside Menger's
work has profound implications for social philosophy in
general. He believes that the "great discovery" of the
classical political economists about the way in which
the market evolves "has become the basis of our
understanding not only of economic life but of most
truly social phenomena" (1948, p. 8). This discovery
is based on the insight that a spontaneous order will
form and maintain itself as a self-correcting order
when individuals are restrained by appropriate rules of
conduct. These rules of conduct are believed to be the
result of a long process of cultural evolution. As a
condition for a self-generating order, such rules,
Hayek emphasizes, were not and cannot be devised by any
one human mind. Individuals instead "stumbled upon"
such rules and their value; the rules themselves
reflect the successful adaptations of past generations.
Civilization, in Hayek's account, should be
regarded as dependent upon the processes of cultural
evolution, in which successful adaptations pass from
one generation to the next. Civilization in this
context is the equivalent of "progress" and refers to
the extensive division of labor and specialization that
makes a higher level of material well-being possible.
To achieve such progress, a coordination of individual
actions in such a way that orderly interaction amongst
them prevails is necessary.

Furthermore, the coordination that has made the "Great Society" of the Western world possible has been largely a byproduct. "[T]he present order of society has largely arisen, not by design, but by the prevalence of the more effective institutions in a process of competition" (1979, p. 154). In various stages of evolution, progressively larger groups of people are brought together. In each stage, the development of basic "tools of civilization"--language, morals, law, and money--facilitates cooperation amongst individuals.

The carrier of these tools through the various stages of civilization is tradition: a body of beliefs and practices which is passed from one generation to the next. As John Gray notes, Hayek's notion of cultural evolution deals entirely with "those rules of action and perception that are not imprinted in the gene" (Gray 1986, p. 109). Hayek's treatment of tradition reflects a basically "functionalist" or adaptationist understanding of culture.

> [C]ulture is man's primary mode of achieving reproductive success. Hence particular sociocultural systems are arrangements of patterned behavior, thought, and feeling that contribute to the survival and reproduction of particular social groups (quoted in Barrett 1984, p. 77).

As Hayek sees it, traditions have been "selected" for their usefulness in coordinating larger groups of people. The people who have survived, then, have done so in large part because of their adherence to favorable traditions.

The other main source of Hayek's approach to understanding cultural evolution comes from Burke, who as I see it combines a functionalist approach with a more reverential attitude. The influence of Burke may account for a certain tone in Hayek's discussion of the process of evolution which is important to recognize for an understanding of his eventual reliance upon cultural evolution to "save the day" for Western civilization. The tone, especially clear in Hayek's essay on "Individualism: True or False" (<u>Individualism and Economic Order</u>, 1948), is one of wonder and humility. Hayek seems in awe of the institutions individual human actions can generate; he is even more humble in front of the "impersonal and anonymous social processes by which individuals help to create things greater than they know" (1948, p. 8). He presents a broad and optimistic vision of the possibilities inherent in the interaction of individuals and social processes. Within the vision is a faith in the vast potential of individual human beings to develop an astounding variety of skills to the greatest possible extent. Man "owes his rapid advance to nothing so much as to the exceptional variety of individual gifts" (1979, p. 173).

This vision is a result of Hayek's effort to blend the political economy of the eighteenth century with what appears to be an almost Burkean conception of an overarching order served by human institutions. This perspective is supported by the appearance in a number of places of language indicative of a belief in some "direction" for evolution. While Hayek's writings on this point are fuzzy rather than clear, it is certain that he thinks it is a marvelous accomplishment that the rules making a Great Society possible evolved in the first place. While he alludes to the possibility that the Great Society may be nothing more than an aberration, he lauds the great growth of individual freedom--and the development of a morality of freedom-- which have made advanced societies possible.

His theory of individualism recognizes the central role played by the purposive individual, but is also and necessarily centered on the idea of structured interaction between individuals, and between individuals and social processes.

> Social processes are understandable only as reconstructions out of individual actions. Collective words such as "class," "state," or "society" do not describe observable entities, and statements containing them only have meaning when translated into statements about individual action (Barry 1981, p. 13).

Hayek's perspective on the relationship between the self and society at this point has elements in common with MacIntyre's view of the situated self, in which individual actions and perceptions are informed by and indeed dependent upon the structures of their culture. It is important to note that Hayek chooses to focus not on the nature of the individual in such a conception, but on the cultural structures that make individual actions comprehensible. Those cultural structures are the result of an evolutionary, impersonal, and anonymous social process.

THE PROCESS OF CULTURAL EVOLUTION

We arrive now at a crucial point in Hayek's argument: his analysis of exactly how the process of cultural evolution takes place. In theories of biological evolution, mutations in a pool of genes supply a variety of combinations from which those best adapted to survival in a given environment are naturally "selected" over time. The criteria for survival vary according to the nature of the environment facing the species. In Hayek's treatment of social evolution, it is variations in traditional "rules of conduct" binding different groups together that supply "mutations" from which successful patterns are selected. Viktor Vanberg summarizes Hayek's focus on cultural evolution as "the notion of the development of rules as an evolutionary process" (1986, p. 76).

The illustration which best supports this view, and the one upon which Hayek appears to rely, postulates the presence of small groups struggling for survival with a minimum of tools in a hostile environment. Groups with rules of conduct that facilitate cooperation and unity, for instance, might survive longer than a factious group. The surviving sets of rules are "chosen" (perhaps through imitation) and passed on to new generations.

At this level of analysis, that of small groups literally struggling for survival, Hayek's account of social evolution seems fairly coherent. It becomes far less clear what criteria of success (or "fitness") are involved in a natural selection process in more advanced civilizations. Reproductive success of the individual will clearly be tied to the entire social system in which the individual resides. Hubert Markl puts this point the following way.

> In a highly evolved social community, an individual's fitness evidently depends on a whole network of multilateral social interactions and multitudinous, long-time behavioral contributions, especially when a system of division of labor exists. This gives the social system emergent characteristics on which an individual's fitness depends in the long run, probably much more so than on its own behavioral endeavors (1980, p. 7).

Up to this point, Markl and Hayek seem to share a common position. Unfortunately for Hayek's position, Markl also points out that just as it is difficult in the case of an individual to identify particular behavioral traits "selected for," ("it is always the whole phenotype that is tested by the environment" [1980, p. 6]) so it is the _entirety_ of the social system that is tested by the (increasingly man-made) environment.

The difficulty for Hayek's concept of cultural evolution is his apparent assumption that cultural traditions so dominate the entirety of the social system that we can believe they are "selected for."

Hayek does of course recognize that government-enforced structures are essential for the development of spontaneous orders like the market, but he does not attempt to assess a whole host of other factors which may contribute to the character of the entire social system. In particular, he fails to specify "the nature, scope, and limits of evolutionary principles and their relation to or interaction with the forces of organized, political choice" (Vanberg 1986, p. 96).

Hayek prefers to emphasize the role traditions as bearers of knowledge play for the continuation of cultural evolution. His analysis of a system of cultural evolution is strikingly similar to Armen Alchian's model of the market as an evolutionary system (1950). Alchian sees the market as a mechanism which selects from many behaviors those conducive to positive profits. What is necessary for the system to function is a set of different actions, from which the relatively better are chosen. In the same manner, for cultural evolution to function, it appears that a wide variety of traditions, or a wide variety of variations within a given tradition, must be practiced. The relatively more successful traditions or variations will survive because the knowledge they contain is conducive to the reproduction of the species. Natural selection amongst competing traditions is to be explained, in part, "by their relative efficiency as bearers or embodiments of knowledge" (Gray 1986, p. 41).

Gray has suggested that one of Hayek's most lasting contributions may in fact be his analysis of social institutions in terms of their ability to generate and use knowledge. Gray is even optimistic enough about this contribution to characterize Hayek's work as representing a "paradigm shift" in social theory, "a shift from the criticism and evaluation of social institutions by reference to preferred principles of morality to an assessment of them in terms of their capacity to generate, transmit and use knowledge (including tacit knowledge)" (1986, p. 41).

While I am doubtful that such a shift has been initiated, I do agree that the emphasis on the knowledge-bearing aspects of evolved institutions is central to understanding Hayek's work. In fact, pursuing this emphasis gives us an insight into Hayek's theory of the good, or the assumptions he makes about desirable and widely shared human ends. Knowledge for Hayek is a shorthand term for a variety of human capacities including skills, dispositions, talents, and practical habits. Hayek's interest in traditions, as in institutions, is how well or poorly they serve to facilitate the fullest possible development of individual human resources.

Does Hayek's perspective on cultural evolution allow us to consider how well or poorly individual development is served? Here the difficulties of his account emerge. His answer to the query is, by definition, that surviving institutions have facilitated the increase of human knowledge in the struggle for survival. This conclusion ignores a large body of anthropological literature that indicates that inefficient and disadvantageous customs may persist for long periods of time.

> [T]he persistence of habit and tradition is such that there is no guarantee that only positive and "neutral" cultural elements survive, or that "if an element actively interferes with efficiency," it will be eliminated....History, as Veblen knew, records numerous instances of the triumph of imbecile institutions over life and culture (Gregg and Williams 1948, p. 602, quoted in Barrett 1984, p. 79).

Hayek's identification of survival with some kind of hidden wisdom distracts us from the reasonable perception that processes of cultural adaptation are never driven exclusively by environmental change. They reflect structural constraints derived from previous cultural patterns as well. In other words, adaptation in a cultural framework never occurs exclusively in ways which enhance human efficiency or reproductive ability. The limited view of human purposiveness as exclusively survivalist I described in Hayek's epistemological theory extends to and dominates his understanding of evolutionary processes.

COMMENTS FROM A SOCIOBIOLOGICAL PERSPECTIVE

Hayek attacks sociobiology in his "The Three Sources of Human Values" (The Political Order of a Free People, 1979) for its failure to distinguish culturally evolved values as apart from innate and "rationally" created values. Yet a number of sophisticated sociobiological accounts do in fact acknowledge the sphere of values Hayek is concerned about. There are striking parallels between Hayek's account and the account of social evolution offered by Lumsden and Wilson, but there are also glaring disparities, particularly in their underlying philosophies. A case in point is the following claim from Charles Lumsden and Edward Wilson's Promethean Fire.

> [A] scientific understanding of human nature and the process of gene-culture coevolution can

provide some measure of intellectual independence from the forces that created us. It can enhance true free will. Real freedom consists of choosing our masters by a procedure that allows us to master them (1983, p. 174).

The contrast with Hayek can be seen starkly when Hayek concludes against counting too greatly on human reason. "Man is not and never will be the master of his fate: his very reason always progresses by leading him into the unknown and unforeseen where he learns new things" (1979, p. 176), but where he certainly does not learn how to "master our masters" (a paradoxical enterprise in any case).

There are three aspects of sociobiological thought that I will discuss in order to place Hayek's understanding of cultural evolution in a clearer perspective. First, I will make some general comments on the validity, from a sociobiological perspective, of assessing morality, and moral traditions, as tools for enhanced survival prospects. I will follow this section with a discussion of the difficulties associated with the idea of "group selection," relying primarily upon Vanberg (1986), who has succinctly related the controversy to Hayek's presentation. Finally, I will examine the position that the demarcation assumed to exist between "innate" and "learned" phenomena (and found in Hayek's work) is far too simplistic to capture the realities of human evolution.

Can morality usefully and accurately be viewed as largely instrumental, in the sense that it is adopted, either unconsciously or consciously, in order to enhance prospects of inclusive fitness? The answer, in general, seems clearly to be negative. Reporting on a set of conference discussions, Markl identifies both the value and the limits of genetically-driven accounts of morality.

An inborn propensity to strive for survival and reproduction has obviously caused man in the past not to disregard the effect of moral norms on fitness. Sociobiological hypotheses about the fitness value of morality are therefore certainly relevant to an understanding of existing moral systems. However, equally clearly, morality transcends the "moral of the genes" by being not inexorably bound to survival as the ultimate value to which any valid moral norm must conform (1980, p. 217).

The survival of the individual or the species as the primary reference for morality has been rejected in

many cultures.   Hayek is frustrated by the willingness
of people to consider morals from a perspective other
than that of survival. For example, he laments what he
regards as the dominant tendency of contemporary
philosophers and scientists who show no particular
inclination to venerate certain norms which Hayek
identifies as being in large part responsible for the
development of the Great Society.

Hayek concludes that the case he makes for
veneration must be a rational one, because while such
normative rules may have evolved spontaneously, to
recover and/or maintain them, it is necessary to
persuade intellectuals of their worth. Advocacy of
morals and the value of moral tradition as it has
evolved over the centuries now requires that that value
be explicated. Gray makes a similar point when he
concludes that if Hayek's "argument about the sort of
morality essential to the stability of the market order
is sound, it has the paradoxical result that a
contemporary conservative who values private property
and individual liberty cannot avoid being an
intellectual and moral radical" (1986, p. 134).
According to Markl, Hayek, by his account of the rise
of morals in aiding group success, cannot avoid
reaching such a conclusion.

> This line of reasoning suggests that morality
> might have arisen as a mechanism increasing the
> fitness of a group in competition with other
> groups, but only on a level of freedom of rational
> reasoning which at the same time opened a way to
> transcend the striving for fitness as an ultimate
> goal (1980, p. 219).

The conclusion of a need for rational explication
of the value of morals, in addition to supplying a
radical twist to Hayek's thought, reinforces his
methodological individualism. Individuals, he implies,
must come to accept that these morals are good for them
as well as good for the Great Society. This
individualist conclusion appears to contradict Hayek's
repeated emphasis on cultural evolution as a "group
selection" process.

Vanberg (1986), after a careful study, concludes
that this emphasis on group selection constitutes a
"major flaw" in Hayek's reasoning and that its
formulation is "too vague to allow for sufficiently
interesting conclusions about the systematic operation
of a group selection process" (1986, pp. 85, 89).
Vanberg briefly notes the controversy in biology about
whether such a thing as group selection can be said to
exist, since it appears in some cases to require a
contradiction of the selective mechanism of Darwinian

evolution (selection according to individual reproductive advantage). The cases in question are those where the individual exhibits "patterns of behavior that, while benefitting the group, appear to be disadvantageous, self-sacrificing on the part of the individuals themselves" (Vanberg 1986, p. 86).

Several comments are in order. First, while Vanberg correctly notes that the scenario for intergroup advantages for self-sacrificing behavior outweighing intragroup disadvantage is thought to occur rarely in nature by biologists, this does not preclude the situation's occurrence in human culture. To say that there may be biological parameters affecting human moralizing, and to draw some conclusions from the study of the evolution of social animals is one thing--but extension of these hypotheses to explanation of human social behavior seems unwarranted. Markl, commenting upon such an explanation, believes the results of sociobiological research are sobering for those "who hope to find the masterkey to an understanding of human social behavior in Sociobiology" (Markl 1980a, p. 9); even in the world of animal sociality, he suggests, biologists are far away from "really understanding what went on and goes on in the evolution of animal sociality" (Markl 1980a, p. 8).

In addition to the dose of skepticism the above theme introduces, it remains the fact that some sociobiologists do dissent from the prevailing doubts about group selection. Donald Campbell summarizes the basis for such a view, noting that "innate tendencies" identified by Robert Trivers may support group altruism. Campbell is relentlessly honest about what such a view presupposes.

> All this is based on the reasonable assumption that life in cooperating social groups increases one's inclusive fitness so greatly over solitary or single-family human existence that there are innate longings for group membership, innate fears of social ostracism, and innate conformity tendencies such as those that favor both the absorption and perpetuation of culture and the coordination of group action (1980, p. 78-79).

Hayek indicates that he tends to believe in such instinctual or innate tendencies--and even though they may have facilitated the evolution of culture (via group selection), he also sees them as serious problems for the further development of the Great Society.

The previous two comments raise the issue of whether morality can be addressed in primarily instrumental terms, which implies that individuals can consciously choose to follow morals. An instrumentalist treatment of morality is consistent with the liberal social contract view of humans as purposive creatures, capable of making choices. Such a view usually conceives of individuals as somehow "extracted" or "abstracted" from the communities or cultures in which they are born and learn from their earliest days. While Hayek recognizes the necessary role played by culture in the development of human reason, he now wishes to argue that certain remnants of our cultural development as social beings must be set aside, dismissed as "atavisms." While this may in some sense be possible for the unencumbered self, it is a different matter for the situated self. For that self, the versions of morality handed down through centuries of cultural evolution contribute to individual identity. As Markl puts it, "by their adherence to a specific set of behavior-regulating rules, members of a culture define themselves" (Markl 1980, p. 217, emphasis added). In addition to the problem of identity which Hayek does not address, another difficulty emerges. In order to claim that our "learned" rules must take precedence over the rules telling us to serve the known needs of known others, Hayek has to regard the former as entirely distinct from the latter. Then he can, at least in theory, suggest that our "innate," inherited, and instinctive tacit knowledge may need to be superseded by our learned tacit knowledge. Can the distinction between "innate" and "learned" be maintained?

Sociobiological studies comment upon the distinction between "innate" and "learned." The essence of this discussion is that we simplify far too readily and without justification when we attempt to maintain such a clear distinction as that which Hayek implies. Roger Masters (1978) draws our attention to several relevant consequences of avoiding the sharp distinction.

First, Masters suggests that different social patterns "are best understood as species-specific adaptations to varied ecological niches" (1978, p. 67). Any social behavior represents an interaction between species and environment, in which both innate and cultural characteristics assume a variety of roles. It is likely to be the case, for example, that cooperative behaviors (or altruistic behaviors) may stem as much from certain innate tendencies (such as those noted above) as from cultural reinforcement of cooperative patterns. In the same way, while innate tendencies may push individuals in competitive directions, it is also the case that cultural traditions can reinforce competitive rather than cooperative behavior.

The second commonsense point that is relevant here is that we should rarely expect to find

biologically-evolved innate instincts serving only one
purpose or directing human behavior down one narrow
path.   Instead, we should expect both considerable
ambivalence on the part of human beings between
reacting with cooperative and competitive behaviors and
behavior which is "multifunctional." The point is that
we cannot successfully dissect human behavior and
classify it in ways which support firm distinctions
between innate and learned, or competitive and
cooperative.   The effect of this perspective, when
combined with the first point from Masters, is that we
should be suspicious of any effort to categorize either
innate   characteristics   or   culturally   acquired
perspectives as "good" or "bad" by definition. Neither
the noble savage nor Hayek's assertion that "[w]hat has
made men good is neither nature nor reason but
tradition" (1979, p. 160) should distract us from
recognizing the complexity of human behavior as a
composite of natural, traditional, and reasoning
influences.
    Hayek's views on cultural evolution, while
provocative, must not be allowed to simplify too
greatly what are complex phenomena.   It is wise, I
think, to conclude this brief foray into
sociobiological theory by looking at two statements
which set limits on how we should assess the validity
of Hayek's emphasis on cultural evolution. The fundamental shape of culturally evolved morality and other
traditions is and will remain biological.

> Biological evolution does not specify what forms
> of social action regulate moral conduct, but it
> defines the boundaries of ethical behavior
> compatible with species survival.   Biology does
> not specify the choices made, but it prepares the
> structural conditions without which there can be
> neither intention or deliberate choice (Wolff
> 1980, p. 92).

Finally, a last ingredient is necessary in order to
assess cultural traditions. This element is implied in
the discussion that the attempt to maintain clear
distinctions between innate versus cultural influences
is inappropriate.   Donald Campbell has put it best:
"[t]he wisdom of any evolutionary process, biological
or social, is wisdom about past worlds" (1979, p. 44).
As a result, where ecological changes have occurred,
there is no reason to presume that previously acquired
traditional knowledge is appropriate.   At some level,
and in some way, evaluations must take place, where the
issue to be decided is whether inherited institutions
are "suitable" for changing times.
    Hayek's position that cultural norms appropriately

repress instinctual tendencies or "primitive" cultural codes related to small group membership represents precisely such a judgement. As I will indicate when discussing "unviable moralities," there may be also an unintended and indeed rarely recognized by-product of "helping" and/or direct meeting of known others' needs that continues to be important in advanced civilizations even if the original motivation for such behavior was survival in the group. This does not have to negate Hayek's emphasis on the destructiveness of a vision of group solidarity around common goals and ways of thinking which can diminish if not destroy individual freedom. Such a vision seduces human beings to the fanaticism the Czech author, Milan Kundera, warns against. The lure to fanaticism is, he says, a dream that is deep within all of us and indeed is expressed in most of the world's religions, a dream of paradise. In this paradise, everyone lives in perfect "harmony, united by a single common will and faith" (1981, p. 233). Hayek's warnings against succumbing to this primitive dream can serve to remind us that not only our dreams but also our inherited traditions require careful evaluation.

CAMPBELL AND HAYEK COMPARED

Hayek cites Campbell's work approvingly in his epilogue on human values (1979). There are two main sources of interest in examining Hayek and Campbell's work together. First, each of them sees a similar function for traditional, evolved rules of conduct. In both accounts, such traditional morals, they believe, serve primarily restraining purposes. The restraint they occasion is useful for restricting human (biological) selfishness, making a cooperative society possible. Campbell, like Hayek, believes that our failure to acknowledge this important function of traditional morals leads us to recklessly disregard what may in fact be extremely critical factors making large societies possible. The desire for "liberation" from such constraints may reduce the options of individuals for choosing the kind of life they wish to live rather than enhancing options. Campbell's 1975 article stirred up an enormous controversy which serves to illustrate the extent to which traditional morals continue to be seen as remnants from which intelligent and rational people can be freed. The dispute is a troubling one, and it appears in other guises in Hayek's work. For example, if individuals are free in a market context where the vast majority of individuals respond to prices they do not understand (a system of rules whose workings they cannot fathom), then is the meaning of freedom subtly changed?

The different ways in which Campbell and Hayek respond to this question of the meaning of freedom indicate a fundamental difference in how they view the use of critical reason by individuals. Hayek, I believe, never clarifies the nature of human agency, and thus never specifies how individuals are free even while connected to the traditions of their society. Campbell, in contrast, is willing to explore the difference between culturally-imposed and self-imposed boundaries. Self-imposed boundaries for freedom do not imply that an individual has plucked boundaries out of some metaphysical heaven; rather, the way in which I think of it is that the individual has engaged in a process of learning, evaluating, and interpreting cultural norms of behavior. Within that framework, the greatest freedom comes within self-accepted boundaries which are regarded as cultural artifacts mediated through the individual's own critical reason. The surface appearance of liberation from all community norms may only open the way for an aimless, meaningless life, in which no choices are seen as particularly worthwhile. On the other hand, an individual engaged in and committed to community norms obtained via tradition, may see himself or herself making difficult choices--but choices which carry genuine and meaningful consequences, so that choosing matters.

The second reason for comparing Hayek and Campbell is that both are, I argue, involved on a similar quest, although Hayek may not recognize that this is so. Both seek what Campbell calls a modest, mediational, scientific kind of normative ethics. Campbell explains the quest in the following way.

> Whatever ultimate norms we choose to live by are the result of presumptive or logically unjustified choices....Once any set of ultimate goals has been decided on by any person or group, a scientific analysis of the status of the world and man's nature can be used to derive mediational ethical and moral rules that are normative, that tell people how to behave, contingent on the assumed ultimate values and on the validity of the scientific analysis of the human condition (1979, p. 37-38).

In order to understand Hayek as a moral philosopher, we must recognize that his intention is also to develop a scientific, mediational ethics.

Hayek presumes, and indeed rarely discusses, that there is a consensus on our ultimate goals which is broadly shared in the Western populations. In his work this set of goals is often referred to as "success" or "prosperity" or "progress" or even increase of numbers of living people. While some people have found this morally bankrupt, it seems to be the case that it is difficult to speak of the fulfillment of human goals unless one presupposes that reproduction is one overriding concern. Hayek assumes another goal, however, which is less well known. This is the existence of a society in which the chance for any randomly taken individual realizing his or her talents and preferences is equal to the chance for any other person. Or as Hayek puts it, "the best society would be that in which we would prefer to place our children if we knew that their position in it would be determined by lot" (1976, p. 132). While this latter goal in particular can mean different things to different people, Hayek appears to believe that it as well as the former goal are broadly presupposed in contemporary discourse.

Given that Hayek accepts these two goals as ultimate goals, and given that he in fact seeks a scientific mediational ethic, then we need to turn to his scientific explanation of human nature and of the world in which we live. To understand modern society, it is not enough to see only the rationally created phenomena, and then dismiss all else as "irrational." Instead, Hayek maintains that observation and analysis should teach us to see both spontaneous and directed orders of events. Once we acknowledge a scientific picture of social institutions as knowledge-bearing structures, then he believes that liberty is the appropriate ethic to pursue.

However, it is in Hayek's scientific analysis of human nature that we find the limits of his ethic of liberty. That ethic reflects the dominance in his thought of the unencumbered view of the self to which we have already alluded. Here his scientific outlook remains firmly anchored within the dominant modern trend, that of refusing to talk about things which we cannot see. Specifically, Hayek refrains from discussing the notion of "meaning," even though his repeated warnings about the dangers of cutting oneself off from the traditions of the Western world would seem to logically prepare the way for discussing meaning. For those traditions contain not only practical knowledge, but practical metaphysics as well. Yet Hayek refuses to acknowledge that this is as least as valuable an aspect of traditional knowledge as is the more practical "how-to" kind of knowledge. Tacit knowledge, in short, is also knowledge about metaphysical questions, and the answers people have constructed which have allowed them to lead relatively satisfying lives. The way in which Hayek's unencumbered view of the self affects his understanding of cultural evolution can be seen in his confusing account of cultural rules and how they change over time.

EVOLUTION AND THE ROLE OF RULES

Hayek thinks about the way in which cultural evolution shapes social life primarily in terms of rules. Rules are the main device by which human beings order their social lives. This position has been described by Norman Barry in the following way: "<u>all</u> social order, continuity, and permanence is explicable only in terms of the notion of rule-following" (Barry 1981, p. 14). To explain social order in terms of the individual requires provision for stable expectations of others' behavior--and rule following allows for such expectations to form. In other words, rules express "patterns of choosing" (Letwin 1976) shared by groups of people. Because such patterns allow people to live together peaceably, rules must be regarded as a prerequisite to civilization.

Rules serve equally important functions for individuals. In any society, "a repertoire of learnt rules" tell individuals "what is the right and what is the wrong way of acting in different circumstances" (Hayek 1979, p. 157). Rules supply guidelines for action and draw upon past experiences of more and less successful kinds of behavior. Every individual born in a society absorbs these rules which guide his or her behavior.

Rules for behavior are regarded by Hayek to be products of cultural evolution embodied in tradition. How does he regard tradition? Geraint Parry argues that all genuine accounts of tradition involve a notion of "custom creeping in sweetly" and without force. Within this range of accounts, he identifies three ways in which political thinkers have viewed tradition over the years. These include Hume's utilitarian view, Burke's vision of tradition as "an insight into the proper ordering of the world," (1982, p. 401), and Oakeshott's understanding of tradition as a "flow of sympathy." Hayek's discussion of tradition seems to encompass each of these perspectives at different points in his writing. In general, though, Hayek may be characterized as viewing tradition as a set of evolved practices or rules within which human reason and individual liberty become meaningful. This is similar to Parry's description of an Oakeshottian view of tradition as "a set of concrete practices pursued because it is only within these practices that any activity can be understood, its problems faced and tackled" (1982, p. 401). Hayek's perspective is broader, for he writes as if the very activity of human reasoning must be placed within traditional rules if we are to gain the fullest understanding possible of human reason.

Evolved traditions supply a necessary background for individual reason. Not only is individual reason, properly understood, embedded in and dependent upon learnt rules, but the development of human reason is dependent upon a social process of growth, "an interpersonal process in which anyone's contribution is tested and corrected by others" (1948, p. 15). Hayek seeks to place reason firmly within the realm of habit, tradition, and experience. Within that realm, human reason is a gift. Outside the limits of that realm, reason becomes dangerous because it then turns into rationalism. Hayek is engaged in a complex appeal to human reason to recognize the organic relationship between individual reason and the social processes at work shaping that reason.

> We must use our reason intelligently, and...in order to do so, we must preserve that indispensable matrix of the uncontrolled and nonrational which is the only environment wherein reason can grow and operate effectively (1960, p. 69).

Hayek's position on the dependence of individual reason on social processes is similar to that of Armen Alchian. Alchian points out that what appear to be customary or nonrational rules of behavior are in fact "codified imitations of observed success" (1950, p. 218). These imitations, many of which are unconscious, are the "matrix of the uncontrolled and nonrational" which Hayek identified as essential for the growth of human reason.

Alchian has also noted that in a changing environment, any one individual cannot compare the results of one action with another. In the market system, for example, "success is discovered by the economic system through a blanketing shotgun process, not by the individual through a converging search" (1950, p. 219). The individual must rely upon the formulas of success embodied in the rules of the game, rules which have value as long as some degree of stability is present.

The development of "social reason" occurs as traditions evolve and change; the reason of any one individual is intertwined with these sources of social reason. To ignore these cultural traditions is to imperil our ability to reason about our world.

What the age of rationalism--and modern
positivism--has taught us to regard as senseless
and meaningless formations due to accident and
caprice, turn out in many instances to be the
foundations on which our capacity for rational
thought rests (Hayek 1979, p. 176).

Traditional rules are the indispensable foundation for
human reason.
     The relationship between tradition and the free
use of reason, or freedom of choice, is far less clear.
Barry in fact argues that Hayek's account "appears to
undermine the autonomy of the individual in the
determination of events" (1984, p. 281). Hayek's
emphasis on rule following is interpreted by others as
contradictory to the notion of free will (see, for
example, Machan 1979, pp. 268-294). The difference
between Hayek and his critics on this point consists of
a different understanding of the role of rules. Do
rules constrain choices, or do they "enable and even
constitute choice?" (Lindgren 1973, p. 57)
     Does Hayek maintain that rules allow individuals
to make choices by structuring alternatives and
facilitating the perception of distinct courses of
action? If so, then rules supply a kind of essential
preparation for choice making analogous to Burkean
"prejudice": "it previously engages the mind in a
steady course of wisdom and virtue, and does not leave
the man hesitating in the moment of decision,
sceptical, puzzled, and unresolved" (Burke 1973, p.
101).
     It is the account of "almost automatic and
necessarily unreflective" (Barry 1984, p. 281) rule
following which convinces me that rules do more than
prepare for choice in Hayek's account. He seems to
ignore or deemphasize two important ways of viewing
traditional rules or knowledge. The first is that any
tradition is dependent upon individual human beings who
"adopt and adapt the practices and beliefs of their
predecessors" (Shils 1981, p. 205). Traditions require
acceptance and sustenance, or they wither and die.
Hayek seems to believe that unconscious beliefs alone
are sufficient. He argues that, "the decisive factors
which will determine that [social] evolution will
always be highly abstract and often unconsciously held
ideas about what is right and proper" (1973, p. 69).
Paradoxically, Hayek himself makes a case for the
adaptation of a certain tradition of viewing liberty,
or in other words, he is trying quite deliberately to
keep a tradition alive.
     The second factor Hayek ignores is even more
puzzling. Despite his emphasis on the importance and
value of individual stores of tacit knowledge, he

writes as if traditional knowledge emerges
"ready-made," available for immediate (and therefore
unreflective) use. It is surely more accurate to
recognize that traditions supply guidelines of a
general nature only.

> But how these general principles should apply in
> any set of concrete circumstances is difficult or
> impossible to specify.... [I]ndividuals always have
> a degree of leeway in the application of cultural
> principles to specific circumstances. They must
> interpret particular situations and choose among
> available alternatives (Barrett 1984, p. 73).

This process of application and choice is
important, because without it, we see neither how
critical reason interacts with traditional knowledge
nor how individuals affect the evolution of that
traditional knowledge. Purposive man is never solely
rule follower, but by this same account he is also
never solely autonomous initiator. Hayek's inability
to incorporate such a perspective in his account of
cultural evolution results, ultimately, in an advocacy
of reverence for tradition that borders upon
resignation.

NORMATIVE IMPLICATIONS DRAWN BY HAYEK

We are now in a position to summarize Hayek's
analysis of the role which cultural evolution plays in
the development of what we think of as a free society.
The rules and institutions of freedom are not the
result of human agency, but of an overarching process
of cultural evolution. Evolved traditions containing
rules of conduct have allowed for the growth of the
market and prosperity for large numbers of people as
well as the development of the human capacity for
rational thought, and with them, the creation of
individual freedom within a free society.
There are, hypothetically, three quite different
normative implications which could be drawn from this
account of the role of cultural evolution. The first
is that people should simply trust that the process of
cultural evolution will continue to make individual
freedom possible. No active role for the individual is
required. Cultural evolution has supplied us a set of
institutions that have brought us progress, and we
should therefore presume that by their very existence,
such institutions are suitable for the time in which we
live. The second is that people can learn from the
processes which brought about a condition that they
value in order to improve upon it and preserve it.

This can be translated into the position that while cultural evolution has done good things for us in the past, we should not assume any enduring structures will continue to prove worthwhile until we discover what advantages and disadvantages they offer.

Part of the confusion about Hayek's thought stems from the fact that he seems to draw both types of implications from his analysis. He does not, however, address a third inference. This is that while there are no patterns to be discerned as models for further efforts to shape cultural institutions, there is a central lesson to be grasped. In the last analysis, the substance of tradition is shaped by how individuals choose to employ their critical reason on a daily basis and at a mundane level. In the remaining pages of this chapter, I will argue the following: (1) in the implications Hayek draws there is a tendency toward advocacy of a blind trust in the forces of evolution; (2) this tendency is expressed most clearly in Hayek's discussion of the evolution of morals; (3) Hayek inconsistently also draws the second implication suggested above, that people can learn from studying the valuable role evolved institutions have played in advanced societies; and (4) had he recognized the role of critical reason in the evolution of tradition, he could have emphasized the third kind of implication and defended his constitutional proposals as a means for guaranteeing the individual liberty in which the daily exercise of critical reason is possible.

Morals and Moral Progress

At a number of points in his discussion of evolution, Hayek creates the impression that the proper implication of his analysis is that there is an inevitable direction in which cultural evolution is pointed, and, furthermore, that the direction is toward a better society. This impression is clearly created in his treatment of morals and moral progress.

Moral rules are themselves a product of evolution.

> The tenets of ethical behavior consist of abstract, general rules.... As I see them, these rules are genuine social growths, the results of a process of evolution and selection, the distilled essence of experiences of which we ourselves have no knowledge (1967, p. 243).

This seems a sensible enough approach to ethical rules: they are rarely devised on the spot, and can be studied in many historical forms. But Hayek goes further: certain rules are "more advanced" than what came

before.   How is "more advanced" defined?   More advanced
rules reflect enhanced survival value.   In effect,
Hayek equates moral advance with the prosperous growth
of a group of people.   "Moral advance by some groups
results from their members adopting rules which are
more conducive to the preservation and welfare of the
group" (1979, p. 155).   Does Hayek mean to say that the
survivors are morally advanced?   As a number of
commentators have indicated, this allows no way for
judging moral worth other than by success--a position
which is weak indeed (Gordon 1981, p. 479).

How does Hayek arrive at this position?   I think
it is the result of an ill-advised generalization from
his study of the Great Society, a society which he
believes is morally advanced.   He suggests that it was
the subjugation of innate instinct to "nonrational
customs which made possible the formation of larger
orderly groups of gradually increasing size" (1979, p.
155).   The first groups within which man lived for
millions of years were small societies or tribes.   In
such small societies, human instincts told individuals
that they must serve the visible needs of known
neighbors and supported the view that common effort for
common ends gave an individual the most satisfaction.
The transition from a tribal society to modern civilization has required the suppression of these instincts
(1979a).

The morals of the Great Society which have slowly
grown to suppress these instincts are the morals of the
market: "[c]ertain abstract rules of honesty--rules
establishing private property and ultimately codified
in the form of private law" (1979a, p. 5).   These
rules, along with an ethic to "pursue a self-chosen end
as effectively as possible" without regard to the needs
of known neighbors, are to guide individual action.   In
Hayek's account, they liberate the individual from the
pursuit of a known common good and allow for a wide
range of individual goals to be pursued.

Is this process of cultural evolution to be
attributed to human actions or supernatural forces of
some kind?   Hayek defends the development over time of
market morals as "moral progress."   But the criteria
for making such a determination are far from clear.
Market morals are those Hayek approves; often he
appears to believe that spontaneous orders will reflect
certain values regardless of the values of the
individuals whose actions produce the orders.   Yet
there are no guarantees that spontaneous evolution will
result in what we think of as a free society (Viner
1961) or that evolved traditions will conform to
liberal principles (Gray 1981).

Is there a more general way to appraise progress?
Is it just the enlarged capacity to support more living

beings?   In this sense, it can be claimed that
institutions selected by evolution will be efficient or
"successful."   Troubling questions persist.   The
meaning of comparative success between advanced
civilizations is difficult to clarify.   Does success
refer simply to survival?   Is this to be survival of
the species, or of a group, or of a civilization?   Or
is there some level of prosperity Hayek has in mind as
indicative of success?   James Buchanan has succinctly
noted in this matter that "there exists a very large
'cushion' between where we are and where we might be
pushed to before species survival might be threatened"
(1982, p. 7).[2]
    Even if we could satisfactorily define the
criteria of success by which institutions are chosen,
we cannot be sure that it is moral traditions alone, or
particular institutions, which determine success.
Perhaps equally important factors are the natural
resource base which allows a society suddenly to leap
from poverty to riches or the will to fight one's
enemies at crucial moments (Diamond 1980).[3]   There is
no particular reason to believe that a system of market
morals will coincide with the former or supply the
latter.
    Perhaps a stronger case can be built around the
role traditions play within a society where a fair
amount of homogeneity and consensus prevail.   Then
traditions may serve a functional role, by protecting a
society from harmful schemes until their beneficial
consequences are proved sufficiently to justify the
overturning of an older tradition.   In a similar way,
Karen Vaughn (1982) suggests the market system based on
private property rules acts to insulate society from
inefficient schemes by requiring the individual to bear
the initial costs of new ventures.
    Without more specific accounts of "success,"
Hayek's admiration for the market order, mixed with his
presentation of the value of evolutionary processes,
leaves the reader with the impression that the
criterion of selection for the process of cultural
evolution may be conduciveness to the Great Society of
Western civilization.   At times Hayek seems to believe
that the inevitable direction of cultural evolution
leads to the market society.   He obviously hopes that
market morals will survive and prosper.
    Hayek's hope is tempered by his own observations
about modern society, observations persuading him that
the survival of market morals is far from assured.   He
knows that many in modern society are repulsed by the
idea that the moral code of the market constitutes
"progress" and recognizes that there are at least two
major costs of the new ethic.   The first is an
emotional void caused by the inability of modern men to

gain the satisfaction of joining a common effort for common ends. This satisfaction simply cannot be maintained on a society-wide base (although within voluntary organizations, for instance, it can be). The second cost is to submit to the discipline of the market, which is also the discipline of freedom: to become more responsible in terms of calculations of the best use to which one can put one's talents and resources. While many individuals rebel against these costs, Hayek remains adamant in his belief that if we want the benefits of the Great Society (ability to maintain life and prosperity of enormously increased population, along with the freedom to pursue individual purposes) then we must pay the costs. Are others so willing to accept the consequences? Hayek is clearly pessimistic.

The Necessity of Resignation?

His fear for the Great Society set of morals leads Hayek into an almost fatalistic attitude toward the ends of cultural evolution: we cannot know the end, but can only trust in history (or some such force). Cultural evolution appears to proceed independently of individual efforts to halt the flow of change.

> Tradition changes but can rarely be deliberately changed....As little as we have designed our whole moral system is it in our power to change it....Ethics is not a matter of choice (1979, pp. 166-167).

Tradition in his most recent works is a force beyond human choice and beyond individual influence.

Earlier in his writings, Hayek does seem to draw the second set of implications, noted above, that human beings can gain valuable insights from the study of evolutionary processes. Traditions, he notes, are tricky things. Not all traditions "are always conducive to success. Some may be retained long after they have outlived their usefulness" (1960, p. 26). Do traditions always function successfully in a broader process, ensuring that a new set of habits must prove its superiority before the old tradition will give way? Neither Hayek nor we can be certain how this works. Traditions are also sometimes accepted because there are no other free choices available. And not all traditions are spontaneously formed nor voluntarily maintained; not all traditions rest upon a consensus in a society. Political debates may in fact be about the content of a particular tradition.

What Hayek at his most optimistic thinks we can

learn is that certain traditions--those on which the
market relies, for instance, as well as traditional
means for controlling government power like the
separation of powers--have facilitated the liberal
society. Once the advantages of evolved institutions
of freedom are recognized, people must attempt to
"perfect and extend the reign of freedom and, for that
purpose, to inquire how a free society" works (1960, p.
54). This is far different from the argument that all
evolved institutions are always to be preserved.

If we focus, for the moment, on the second set of
implications about cultural evolution, we still
confront a dilemma. How do we know that we have
learned "enough" to tamper with evolved institutions?
The question then becomes: when are we to rely on
evolved traditions, and when must we attempt to alter
or form traditions and institutions? In other words,
when is rational design indicated? Hayek's own
epistemological skepticism argues against finding
conclusive evidence to suggest that a clearly
appropriate occasion for innovation has presented
itself.

Yet practical, everyday use of critical reason is
part of a continuous exercise of judgement that is
culturally conditioned. Hayek's apparent plea for
recognition of the past (rather than resignation to it)
is strikingly similar to the concept of "character"
employed by Michael Sandel. For Sandel, to have
character is to "know that I move in a history I
neither summon nor command, which carries consequences
none the less for my choices and conduct" (1982, p.
179). Hayek has no basis for expecting such character
due to the central presence in his work of an
unencumbered model of the self, the self pursuing
"self-chosen" ends.

In Sandel's account, character for the confidently
situated self arises in part from recognition of one's
identity as social in nature, an identity intertwined
with that of the cultural community of which one is a
part. Hayek provides neither the assumptions nor the
language to express such realization of identity.
Therefore, having removed individuals from any sense of
"story," and relying upon "the identification of
individual interests...prior to, and independent of,
the construction of any moral or social bonds between
them" (Sandel 1984, p. 250), Hayek is understandably
puzzled about how a sense of tradition can be acquired
in a market society. Failing to see the potential
already in place for individuals to recapture the kind
of appreciation of our cultural heritage he believes
essential for the preservation of a liberal society,
Hayek turns increasingly to an invocation of
supernatural forces--those of cultural evolution--for

our salvation.   The underlying concern for ordered
liberty has <u>not</u> changed, but Hayek's faith in human
agency has.   With a satisfactorily revised
understanding of the self and human agency, advocacy of
ordered liberty need not have ended in a call for
conservatism.

NOTES

1.   Perhaps the most famous statement of this position
      is found in Burke's <u>Reflections on the Revolution</u>
      <u>in France</u> (1973, p. 74):

           It is with infinite caution that any man
           ought to venture upon pulling down an edifice
           which has answered in any tolerable degree
           for ages the common purposes of society, or
           on building it up again, without having
           models and patterns of approved utility
           before his eyes.

2.   I would like to thank Professor Buchanan for
      supplying me with a copy of his unpublished paper,
      "Cultural Evolution and Institutional Reform,"
      which addresses the same paradox identified in
      this study.
3.   One thinks immediately of a country like Saudi
      Arabia, where oil-based wealth has produced
      enormous development and prosperity in a very
      short time span.

☆ 4 ☆
Explaining the Contradiction in Hayek's Thought

As the preceding chapters demonstrate, Hayek's keen appreciation of the value of evolved social products does not prevent him from setting forth a radical plan for redesigning democratic institutions. His skeptical distrust of rationalism and preference for relying upon the accumulation of experience expressed in surviving social structures is not applied when he examines political institutions. As a result, his position is clearly distinct from that of Edward Banfield, a contemporary American skeptic. Banfield views political institutions in the following way.

> A political system is an accident. It is an accumulation of habits, customs, prejudices and principles that have survived a long progress of trial and error and of ceaseless response to changing circumstance... To meddle with the structure and operation of a successful political system is therefore the greatest foolishness that men are capable of. Because the system is intricate beyond comprehension, the chance of improving it in the ways intended is slight, whereas the danger of disturbing its working and of setting off a succession of unwanted effects that will extend throughout the whole society is great (Banfield 1964, pp. 37-38).

Hayek's overall skepticism and cultural conservatism are at odds with the critical rationalist direction that his constitutional proposals impart to his political philosophy. How are we to account for the striking inconsistency?

I argue that the best way to account for his simultaneous veneration of tradition and his excursion into constitutional engineering is to see that they are rooted in his rich and complex understanding of ordered

liberty.   In part because of the density of Hayek's
writings,   there   is   considerable   material   for
alternative   explanations   of   the   discrepancy   between
central themes in his thought.   In this chapter I set
out in summary form and then explore three alternative
accounts.   The three accounts, along with my own as a
fourth, can be presented in the following way.

1. The contradiction identified in this book is
   a   simple   reflection   of   the   fundamental
   incoherence of his thought.   The incoherence
   reveals itself in two ways.   The first is his
   attraction   to   both   liberalism   and
   conservatism; the second is his difficulty in
   clarifying the definitions of some key terms
   in his argument.

2. The   contradiction   in   Hayek's   philosophy
   reflects his ultimate preoccupation with the
   idea   of   progress.   His   commitment   to   the
   notion   of   progress,   rather   than   liberty,
   accounts for his inconsistent positions and
   leaves   him   vulnerable   to   charges   of   moral
   relativism.

3. The inconsistency arises from Hayek's effort
   to defend and justify the "free market."   His
   interest   in   cultural   evolution   developed
   solely from his perception that it played a
   role   in   the   development   of   the   market
   society,   but   once   he   recognized   that
   preservation   of   that   society   rested   upon
   politics,   he   became   a   constructivist
   rationalist.

4. The   contradiction   in   Hayek's   thought   arises
   from his rich and complex but nevertheless
   flawed   account   of   the   nature   of   ordered
   liberty.   His incomplete understanding of the
   self   provides   him   no   coherent   basis   for
   explaining why both veneration of traditional
   knowledge   and   willingness   to   defend
   individual liberty through political means
   are required.

The first three alternatives set out represent my
own   distillation   of   the   work   of   a   number   of
contemporary Hayek scholars, some of whom might object
to the way in which I have categorized their work.   My
goal   here   is   not   to   attack   or   defend   particular
interpretations of Hayek's work.   Instead, I explore
the   first   three   alternatives   in   order   to   show   that
while   each   has   some   validity   for   explaining   parts   of
Hayek's work,   each   in   turn   raises   other   difficulties
for   their   explanatory   scheme   which   my   own   explanation
can resolve.

Each of the four explanations accounts for Hayek's constitutional design in different ways. The first recognizes Hayek's reverence for evolved institutions but claims that his definition of what constitutes an evolved institution is problematic. In this account, the presence of his reverence alongside constitutional engineering is held to reflect his attraction to both liberal and conservative philosophies. His willingness to redesign political institutions then appears consistent in Hayek's mind only because either the definitional slack allows him to believe that political products are not evolved orders as he defines them, or he unknowingly shifts gears between philosophical approaches. Whether such a definitional problem exists, and whether it explains the discordant note between his general philosophy and his political thought will be discussed below.

The second explanation emphasizes that Hayek's interest in cultural evolution is centered around discovering the roles played by particular institutions in achieving progress. His primary goal is economic growth or material progress spurred by economic growth. Liberty, as well as the processes of cultural evolution, is embraced only to the extent that he sees each as necessary for the generation of such progress. When social or political analysis reveals some development in morals or politics threatens the further pursuit of progress, Hayek has no choice but to argue for reform.

In the third account Hayek is seen as a defender of the status quo, which includes a defense of the market society, but not on the grounds of progress so much as on the grounds that the market society is the best possible kind of society we have yet beheld. Other values he might hold are subordinate to his hostility to socialistic alternatives to the market society. Political systems have a key role to play in protecting and perpetuating the market society, and constitutional design becomes a means for reform of the political system in ways more compatible with the market.

I have reserved discussion of the fourth premise for the next chapter. I will argue there that this last premise fits the whole of Hayek's philosophy better than the other three. It supplies, however, only a partly satisfactory resolution to the inconsistency between his traditionalism and his constitutional engineering. The critical point upon which political institutions and their role in the overall order of the Great Society are judged is liberty: the extent to which an institution sustains and is conducive to individual freedom. Because political institutions play a vital and necessary (though not sufficient) role in creating a space for ordered liberty, if one of them is shown to be infringing upon or threatening freedom, then it would be paradoxical not to call for reform of such an institution. Arriving at this assessment of Hayek's treatment of political institutions indicates that our evaluation of his overall philosophy, and particularly his prescriptive political philosophy, must rest upon what we think of his understanding of liberty. Before turning to that task, I will establish why the first three accounts are less appropriate vehicles for assessing the whole of Hayek's work.

COSMOS VERSUS TAXIS

        Hayek is attracted to two different political philosophies:

        classical liberalism (based on limited government, free markets, and the rule of law) and a conservative philosophy which stresses tradition and the hidden wisdom of existing institutions (Brittan, 1983, p. 54).

In this manner, Samuel Brittan suggests that we view Hayek as a philosopher whose basic loyalties are in question. Norman Barry concludes his most recent article on Hayek in a similar way. It is not, says Barry, that there is some superficial unity beneath which lurks a "mass of contradictions. It is rather that the 'hard' liberalism of his economic philosophy forms a kind of carapace beneath which a [philosophical] doctrine of tradition is very much alive" (1984, p. 285).

        The theme of an underlying contradiction incapable of resolution is echoed in the position that Hayek faces a fundamental terminological dilemma when he attempts to clearly distinguish between a "cosmos" and a "taxis." It is with these terms that he seeks to clarify whether an institution represents an "evolved order." A cosmos is defined as a recognizable order which has not been designed by any one individual and consequently has no purpose. An order is not the same as an equilibrium; an order exists in spite of and in the midst of the changing processes by which individual needs are met. An order is a "condition of affairs in which we can successfully form expectations and hypotheses about the future" (1978, p. 73). Regularities exist in sufficient quantity to allow individuals reasonable bases on which to plan. This kind of order is a prerequisite for rational behavior (i.e., without regularities upon which to shape expectations, purposive individuals could not form plans).

The order of the cosmos depends upon the observance of "nomoi," universal and abstract rules of conduct. Individual actions, Hayek contends, need not be consciously directed toward creating or maintaining the cosmos. The key element is that these individuals are following certain rules, rules which may but need not be articulated, even by those observing them. The real function of rules is, however, adaptive. With only limited knowledge, individuals must accept that they cannot always know why certain rules are followed. An illustration of this can be drawn from the field of language. Learning a foreign language requires the student to follow often complex sets of rules which natives of the language follow without question. No particular reasons are known to most individuals (nor do they usually speak as though they feel "constrained" by such rules); the result, however, is communication via the use of a shared language based on rules of grammar.

The opposite of cosmos is taxis, or organization. An organization is a deliberate arrangement devised by men and women with a particular purpose in mind. A design, a conscious human invention makes taxis possible. The continued existence of a taxis rests upon the issuance and observance of theses or particular commands. Many activities, including a wide range of voluntary activities are carried out in organizations. A taxis, as opposed to a cosmos, does not appear as a by-product of the observance of general rules.

The distinction between cosmos and taxis lies at the heart of Hayek's political theory. Society itself is a cosmos which contains, among many other organizations, the organization called "government." While society rests upon a slowly developed set of abstract rules of conduct, government was instituted for a purpose; originally the purpose was to enforce learned principles of conduct. While Hayek admits that the accepted purposes of a government must change to some extent with the passage of time, the recognition that government is instituted for a particular purpose is important in his political theory. The legitimacy of government action is limited. A yardstick is implicitly available for measuring that legitimacy: if government activities exceed those necessary to fulfill the stated purpose, then they are illegitimate. Control of Leviathan is legitimated and required by this distinction between cosmos and taxis.

The definition of government as taxis also conveys a notion of dependency to government. The ongoing business of everyday life occurs in the cosmos--the

core of human life is located there. While government
may facilitate or impede the everyday activities of
social life, government as an organization can be
regarded as a transitory phenomenon. "Whatever the
changing structure of government, the basic structure
of society resting on the rules of conduct persists"
(1978, p. 78). Governments come and go, but societies
endure.

The distinction between cosmos and taxis sounds
plausible on first examination. There is no evidence,
however, that Hayek intends to make the claim that when
a taxis infringes upon the spontaneous order of cosmos,
constructivist reform of the organization in question
is justified. This would be a radical claim indeed.
Nor does he invoke the distinction to account for his
willingness to advocate reform of government. This is
prudent, for despite his carefully drawn distinction
between taxis and cosmos, he himself sometimes speaks
of government as a product of factors other than
design. For instance, he acknowledges that existing
governmental systems may reflect as much accidents of
history and interpretations of history as overtly
designed constitutions (1960, p. 183). At the very
least, a taxis may be regarded as an unintended product
of intentional actions.

Hayek may have recognized that the distinction
between cosmos and taxis, while useful in certain
didactic senses, is not precise enough to serve as a
boundary for the proper subjects of human design. The
boundaries between organizations and spontaneous orders
are very difficult to identify. As Karen Vaughn
concludes, "a 'spontaneous order' develops within the
structure of government which in many instances runs
contrary to the stated purposes of the organizations.
Indeed that is the theme of the most Public Choice
literature" (1982, p. 13).[1]

A further difficulty in identifying such
boundaries is related to the nature of the rules on
which a spontaneous order rests. Hayek alludes to the
possibility that a spontaneous order "may rest in part
on regularities which are not spontaneous but imposed"
(1978, pp. 74-75). If the regularities are imposed,
does the order remain spontaneous? Richard Vernon,
considering this possibility, asks, "If a spontaneous
order depends upon political enforcement is it then
spontaneous?" (1976, p. 266). In a similar way, J.C.
Rees maintains that to hold interference with the
cosmos to be harmful or dangerous implies "that we can
ascribe certain consequences to deliberate intervention
and compare the resulting situation with what it would
otherwise have been" (1963, p. 350). While the concept
of "undesigned" cosmos is helpful for combatting
constructivist fallacies, maintaining strong

distinctions between it and taxis must rest upon both
knowledge Hayek doubts we have, as a rule, and the
application of certain values.

The fuzzy nature of the distinction between cosmos
and taxis appears to me to be the base for the claim
made by Roger Arnold that, appearances to the contrary,
Hayek's position is "not, at base, a commendation of
the evolutionary process" (1980, p. 342). Instead, he
sees Hayek defending outcomes resulting from evolution
in the context of a specified environment. Only within
certain specified environments does Hayek expect the
resulting order to be valuable. Apparently, Arnold
concludes that Hayek sees the growth of cosmos to be
dependent upon (constructed) taxis. Thus Arnold calls
Hayek a "non-teleological constructivist." His
willingness to tamper with political structures
represents a _consistent_ application of his selected
approval of evolutionary processes. The specified
environment in which evolutionary processes are
approved, according to Arnold, is one in which
adherence to an abstract moral code on the part of
individuals complements the presence of both
competition guided by general rules and individual
liberty. If competition, for example, is undermined by
governmental action, then Hayek would be committed to
rectifying the situation "non-teleologically," in order
to facilitate the continuation of acceptable
evolutionary processes.

Arnold's argument, while interesting, appears to
ignore Hayek's clear demonstration of support for the
evolutionary processes by which social tools like law
and morals have developed. In his account, Hayek
indicates that the first steps making the Great Society
of general rules and individual liberty possible were
taken by law breakers. The development of law and
morals presupposed neither an abstract moral code which
all involved supported nor any institutional guarantees
of individual liberty. Yet Hayek applauds the slow
development which occurred in both areas.

What Arnold's confusion reveals is the extent to
which Hayek has modelled his concept of cosmos on the
example of the market. The conditions Arnold discusses
are in fact those which Hayek sees as necessary for the
market to function in an optimal manner. It may be the
case that the best example of a cosmos, and perhaps the
only clearcut one, is the institution of the market.
The market is one strong pole of Hayek's philosophy,
around which he builds in and tries to fit other
elements. This brings us back full circle to Barry's
observation that Hayek's "philosophical accompaniment"
to economic rationalism involves him in inescapable
inconsistencies.

This perspective on Hayek ultimately does _not_

explain the inconsistency other than by attempting to persuade us that despite Hayek's considerable accomplishments, his work is seriously flawed. But there is, I think, an implied contention that the central value of Hayek is the market, rather than any particular philosophical orientation and an implied criticism that he fails to confront the consequences of his commitment to the market. In my interpretation, I contend that it is less the consequences of commitment to the market and more the consequences of the concept of the self for whom he envisions ordered liberty that Hayek fails to understand.

LIBERTY FOR PROGRESS

The second explanation of the contradiction in Hayek's thought views that contradiction as an indication of the centrality in his work of the idea of progress. Brittan comments lucidly that by progress Hayek means "movement and increase of complexity (in the biological sense)...the 'evolution of the human race'" (1983, p. 53). Rees suggests that the "individual's right to experiment and to adopt new practices is derived from the need to harness the unique talents of every potential innovator in the cause of social progress" (1963, p. 351). This set of explanations emphasizes that Hayek evaluates all institutions in terms of how they contribute to the evolution of the human species or progress as he understands it. In his account, there must be some way in which we can understand how certain institutions and processes contribute to human progress. Working from those insights, we can criticize certain features of society or government as detrimental to progress.

The examples used by Hayek suggest that he suspects that centralized and collectively-generated as opposed to decentralized and individually-generated choices may be predisposed to have negative consequences for human progress. This provides one avenue for understanding his defense of the products of evolution arising from many individual decisions (as in the market, at least theoretically speaking) which contribute to the ongoing order of Western society, while seeking reform of the products of evolution resulting from primarily collective choices (as in legislative rule making) which harm that order. Here we encounter familiar problems: just as the distinction between spontaneous order and organization breaks down upon close analysis, so too does some kind of absolute dividing line between individualized (market) and collectivized (political) choices.

In general, the consequences of collective

decision making loom larger, last longer, and have more
unexpected consequences (because of limitations of
social knowledge) than do those of individual decision
making.   In other words, collective processes may
affect evolution adversely because the negative
consequences cannot be isolated on a smaller (i.e.,
individual) scale than that of entire societies. Where
such isolation is possible, negative effects harm small
numbers of individuals, while positive effects become
readily available for imitation and development.

Working from this second premise allows us to view
Hayek as arguing in favor of evolutionary processes for
their progressive consequences, while retaining the
position that not all evolutionary processes will
necessarily generate features conducive to progress.
Particularly in collective contexts, where government
actions mingle with individual acts in the "gene pool"
of cultural change, we are not to believe that good
outcomes in the sense of progressive outcomes, will
always arise. Does this explanation allow us to make
sense of Hayek's work?

Two objections to its use for this purpose may be
raised. First, it could be argued that, as long as a
variety of collective actors are making decisions
(supplying mutations), the process of evolution will
continue to select the relatively "better" mutations.
As long as different political units are available,
then the processes of imitation and selection will
continue to take place. The time frame may be longer,
and the costs to individuals higher or more widespread,
but the selection to preserve the species will
continue.   Since a variety of collective
decision-making units (towns, cities, states) do exist
in precisely the democratic societies Hayek wants to
reform, it is not at all clear from this premise why he
is not content to let the process unfold. If anything,
this premise would seem to lead to suggestions for
disaggregating government rather than strengthening
central governmental institutions.

The second objection is more obvious than the
first. An evaluation of "bad" versus "good" evolution
requires judgement according to values. To say that
collectively-generated options impede human
adaptability implies at least that change is valued--
and that we can foresee future developments.[2] In fact,
short of extreme cases where certain mutations will
obviously destroy the human species, given the
limitations of human knowledge, it is difficult to
predict the effects of any mutation in advance. To go
further and say that collectively-generated mutations
are more likely to be harmful than individually-
generated ones implies a concern for specific values.
Once this is acknowledged, it is necessary to examine

those values rather than the broader topic of progress as the central focus in Hayek's work.

Case Study: The Generation of Unviable Moralities

My argument that specific values rather than a concern for the evolution of the human species informs Hayek's work can be illustrated by looking at his discussion of unviable moralities. John Gray has illustrated "how within the critical rationalist framework of Hayek's doctrine, judgements may be made condemning large segments of inherited and contemporary moral life as incompatible with the market order to which mankind owes its present numbers" (1986, pp. 132-133) by examining Hayek's discussion of "unviable moralities." Gray defines these along Polanyian lines, as "forms of moral life destructive of the very societies in which they are practiced" (1986, p. 133). A careful look at Hayek's discussion of unviable moralities in particular and of morality in general reveals that the argument for progress is in reality an argument about the importance of certain values.

First, there are some fundamental difficulties centering around what I now believe is Hayek's incorrect assessment of the nature of morality in market societies. Examining his assessment leads us into an assessment of the "scientific" nature of his argument for progress. When we dig carefully into Hayek's view of what we know about the factors which lead to progress, we find far less "knowledge" and far more a set of value judgements. Thus Hayek cannot, and does not, give us any peculiar insights into how we progress (which, in actuality is consistent with his general epistemological stance, that we progress in ways we cannot foresee), but he makes an impassioned plea in the name of certain values. To regard his political philosophy as based upon this second premise, then, is to misinterpret (in ways facilitated by Hayek's presentation) what is an argument in favor of certain values, certain ways of living for human beings. Hayek does not give us a scientific explication of the necessary elements of progress; he gives us a picture of what human life should be about. The human life he values in this context is one in which people are truly unencumbered selves, freely responding to abstract price signals in market settings, and thereby making the best possible use of their individual talents.

The primary focus of Hayek's discussion of unviable moralities is on the resurgence of what he considers to be "tribal ethics," deeply ingrained instincts which human beings inherited genetically during centuries of existence in small bands. The "morality" (if we can call it that) of these groups of human beings centered around directing individuals toward common visible purposes. These purposes revolved around meeting the "known needs of known other people" (1983, p. 31), which Hayek seems to acknowledge gave to individuals both a sense of completing satisfying tasks and the assurance that in case of need, support would be forthcoming. This "morality," in other words, was emotionally satisfying, serving group needs while at the same time serving the individual.

While an initial reading of Hayek on morals seems to indicate that individuals must simply accept that tribal ethics have no role to play in a market society, further reading indicates that this is not the case. For while Hayek's emphasis is on the "market morals" which he fears contemporary societies are attempting to abandon, he also makes a number of comments about the role which tribal ethics continue to play even in an Open Society. These "primordial" emotions are required in special personal relations, small groups, and voluntary organizations. In his discussion of the "irreplaceable values" which positivism denigrates, he chides positivists for failing to see "that even emotional responses selected by biological or cultural evolution may be of the greatest importance for the coherence of an advanced society" (1979, p. 173).

Hayek even goes so far as to acknowledge that the transition from tribal ethics, or what I will from now on term "particularistic morals," to market morals has left an "emotional void" (1983, pp. 42-43). This is the fertile soil in which an "unviable morality" has grown. It is characterized by the desire for the bond of pursuit of common goals with others, often emerging in calls for "social justice." Because of the emotional void, individuals are in a sense "primed" to hear the messages of psychiatrists and prophets alike, urging them to reject a world which fails to satisfy their deepest "natural" desires.[3]

An additional element appears, in Hayek's mind, to have facilitated an inappropriate resurgence of particularistic morals. This is the fact that many people in an advanced industrial society do not interact with the market as producers, because their livelihood is earned within an organization. The organization in effect serves to mediate between the individual and the market. I am increasingly doubtful that this is a helpful way to view the relationship of contemporary people to the market. When market changes occur, and organizations lay off employees, for example, the interaction with the market is directly experienced. Hayek contrasts contemporary employees with peasants, craftsmen, and merchants, commenting at one point that the morals of the market were accepted as "a matter of course" (1983, p. 33) by these kinds of people. As members of organizations, Hayek seems to complain, people fail to see the "superiority of blind obedience to abstract rules" which the market requires and may even be tempted to abandon the moral ethic of the market, which is to pursue individual gain without regard for the consequences that pursuit may have in the complex network of human activities. The particularistic morals of responding to known needs of known individuals within organizations tend to overpower the "universal morals" upon which the market and the Open Society rest.

Is Hayek's alarm justified? It is certainly the case that groups of individuals sharing particularistic morals have committed some atrocities in the history of humankind--but so too have individuals with more universalistic morals. The alarm for the future of the market in terms of morals is not justified, however, in terms of the account of unviable morality Hayek has given us. This is because he has attempted to draw a clear-cut distinction between particularistic and universal morals. By attempting to make the distinction, Hayek oversimplifies the tribal existence and deprives himself and us of understanding a fundamental element of human freedom. Paradoxically, the vast majority of Hayek's work exemplifies the approach of a person who does understand this fundamental element of human freedom.

The element of freedom to which I refer is that of making moral choices. As has been noted earlier, the emphasis on rule following in Hayek's work tends to obscure a role for individual choice. Tom Kitwood (1983) comments that "having to make choices and take responsibility...is one of the most valid ways in which we assert our freedom" (p. 228-229). He goes on to outline what I think is a more helpful understanding of the human moral condition: human beings confront opposing commitments and always have done so.

> [T]here now exists a fundamental tension between universalistic and particularistic ethical claims....The tension has always existed to some extent. Even "primitive" people had to decide how to treat the "stranger," whether as a non-person or as a human being like themselves....To be morally aware in the modern world is to recognize this tension and to live with it...(1983, p. 228).

What may be said to alarm Hayek, then, is that a great many people seem to be living with the tension by favoring particularistic ethics at the expense of the universal ethics upon which he believes the market rests.

What exactly are the ethics upon which the market rests? Despite Hayek's emphasis on the cultural foundations of human reason and human existence, there seems to me to be a curious lapse in his discussion of the morals upon which the market draws. The lapse is both a product of the effort to draw clear distinctions noted above and an indication of the grave shortcomings of Hayek's working within the paradigm of the unencumbered self. The lapse is revealed in two ways. One is that he does not discuss market morals in terms of our understanding that the market is always dependent "on all the complex and particular social relations in which it exists" (Macneil 1986, p. 593, emphasis added). In other words, in general, the market rests upon not just market morals but also the particularistic morals of earlier societies. The second way in which the lapse appears is when he discusses the morals of the market primarily resting upon property and family. This is a curiously circumscribed definition of morals, once we recognize that morals "almost always involve family duties, duties of friendship, duties in respect of money and property" and involve recognition of one's shared humanity (Vine 1983, p. 30).

To what can we attribute the attenuated definition? Is Hayek unaware of friendship and awareness of shared humanity? Is it that he assumes (with a great many liberals) that this is the background against which individuality develops, and he chooses to focus on the foreground rather than the background? Yet a great deal of his writing has to do with precisely the backdrop to individual actions which we often fail to consider.

The attenuated definition reflects Hayek's inability to conceive fully of individuals as situated selves. By viewing people as unencumbered selves, he avoids the problematic nature of these very moral duties (friendship, shared sense of humanity) for individuals in contemporary market societies. The concept of an "unviable morality" can be employed to examine certain disturbing implications of Hayek's account of market morals. To see this, we need to look closely at his understanding of the basis of morals and at what market morals require of individuals. Morals, he contends, rest upon the "esteem" of one's fellows, who evaluate one's striving for excellence and recognize one's achievements (1979, p. 171). In the context of the small band, esteem was facilitated by everyone's recognition of "accepted patterns of life-history" and repeated interactions with the group, in which the nature of the individual became known to the social group (Kitwood, 1983, p. 220).

In the market society, according to Hayek, esteem can no longer rest upon one's pursuit of a known common good. Instead, the "prudent man," one who built up capital was esteemed, or, in short, financial gain became the criterion by which one's morality was assessed. "Financial gain rather than the pursuit of a known common good became...the basis of approval" (1979, p. 165). Yet Hayek himself speaks of the market, the catallactic order, as a game of chance! Esteem based upon financial gain alone becomes extremely difficult to distinguish from esteem based upon luck. On what basis, then, in an abstract rather than person-to-person society, can judgements of moral worth be made? This is a confusing and perplexing matter on which rests a great deal of the turmoil of modern society. The strangers with whom one interacts in a market society, according to market morals, must remain fundamentally unesteemable--we must give up the illusion that we can evaluate them. Yet does the amoral conclusion this implies provide a satisfactory basis for the preservation of advanced Western societies?

I argue that market morals alone can not provide a satisfactory basis for reproduction of the extensive social relations upon which the market and Western civilization is dependent. Hayek acknowledges the neoconservative position on this matter and appears on occasion to intuitively grope toward a genuine solution. In a footnote, he quotes approvingly from de Jouvenal that while man cannot hope to turn a large society into a small community, man "undoubtedly goes to [the small community] to renew his strength" (1976, p. 191, n. 15). Elsewhere, Hayek laments the fact that people "lack patience and faith" to build up voluntary organizations for purposes we highly value.

What he fails to see is that part of the "unviability" of market morals is that they not only cast the basis for esteem of others in doubt, but that the overwhelming and seductive nature of market language and interactions tends to devalue extramarket, social activities. Ultimately, moral judgements of any kind of activity become secondary to the position that what "succeeds" is good. Purposes neither readily satisfied in market settings nor measured by success cannot be judged by the all-pervasive market morals. A society driven by the morality of the market will be "lacking in any compelling moral content" because such a society "can in the end only identify the good with that which prevails" (Gray 1986, p. 142). In Hayek's account, the ordered liberty based on the morals of the market he values so highly appears doomed to crumble for lack of moral justification. Ironically, had his

account of morality been shaped by perceptions of
people as situated selves, Hayek might have been far
more optimistic about the prospects for the
perpetuation of human liberty and market economies.

THE MYTH OF THE MARKET

     The third alternative for explaining Hayek's work
is that Hayek judges political institutions according
to how they affect the workings of the market society.
Of the accounts we have looked at so far, this one has
by far the best textual evidence. Hayek's admiration
for the market as a coordinating mechanism is well
known. What is less well known is the elaborate theory
of the market and its relationship to a free society
which he has developed around the term, "catallaxy."
     A catallaxy can be defined clearly as "the special
kind of spontaneous order produced by the market
through people acting within the rules of the law of
property, tort, and contract" (1976, p. 109). The
catallaxy is in fact the phenomenon on which Hayek's
broader set of spontaneous or self-generating orders is
modelled. The vital role which catallaxy plays in
Hayek's philosophy is demonstrated in a remarkable
passage where he sets forth one of the principles he
believes to be supported by past experience.

     The truth is that catallactics is the science
     which describes the only overall order that
     comprehends nearly all mankind, and that the
     economist is therefore entitled to insist that
     conduciveness to that order be accepted as a
     standard by which all particular institutions are
     judged (1976, p. 113).

     The catallaxy is alleged to produce three
indispensable elements of civilization: wealth,
progress, and peaceful cooperation. In each case, the
emphasis is on social products rather than on
individual development. Hayek stresses the fact that
the market "serves to elicit from each player the
highest worthwhile contribution to the common pool"
(1979b, p. 7). Particular individuals will be
disappointed, will fail, will suffer; yet because the
catallaxy assures the best chance for any person taken
at random to live a good life in a civilized society,
it is to be supported. It is not that Hayek's
allegiance has changed from the individual to the
social order; it is rather that he sees that a concern
for individual development requires concern for the
social context in which any given individual must move.
The catallaxy allows civilization to flourish.

Hayek goes even further to assert that wherever a Great Society has arisen, it has been made possible by a system of rules of conduct including the law of property, tort, and contract (1976, p. 40). It would seem worthwhile to undertake a systematic, comparative study of the laws of thriving civilizations to see whether such an assertion could be confirmed. Short of such confirmation, we can at least explore each of the elements of civilization Hayek claims a catallaxy generates.

The examination of the first two factors, wealth and progress, need not be detailed. It seems to me that it is widely accepted that a catallactic order facilitates the generation of wealth on a scale which any other economic order has yet to match. Whether this is regarded as good or bad, it seems difficult to argue against the basic statement. Competition and the incentives provided by a market order to entrepreneurs also serve to encourage the discovery of new knowledge which leads to human progress. Knowledge and particularly the accumulation of changing knowledge play a vital role in Hayek's understanding of the market. This is a central tenet of the Austrian economic tradition. "The market process is the outward manifestation of an unending stream of knowledge" (Lachmann 1976, p. 127). It is essential to note once more that a catallaxy does not just "happen" but rests on rules which must be continually redefined and enforced. Increases in a society's total wealth and the accumulation of knowledge depend upon the content of those rules.

The third element Hayek claims is generated by the market I have called peaceful cooperation. One of the fundamental differences between supporters and opponents of the market order rests on a perception of whether conflict or cooperation prevails in a market society. Many opponents of the market seem to believe that the Hobbesian jungle is in fact present in a catallaxy, but restrained (precariously) by government coercion. Exploitation and barely concealed hostility are the general rule. Supporters of the catallaxy, on the other hand, point out that many individuals exchange certain goods for others, expressing satisfaction with the outcomes in a courteous and civilized manner.

There are two parts to Hayek's support of the market in terms of peaceful cooperation. Neither is widely understood. The first is caught in one definition of the Greek word for bartering or exchanging, katalattein. "In addition to 'exchanging' it also meant 'to admit into the community' and 'to change from enemy into friend'" (1979a, p. 6). In Hayek's version of the development of civilization, he seems to be thinking of cases where confiscation and raiding are replaced by exchange, and it is possible for warring neighbors to become peaceable ones. Coerced exchange is rightly to be regarded as but another variant of confiscation; but free exchange involves mutual benefit.[4] Perceptions of mutual benefit allow the reconciliation of different individual purposes. The result is that peaceful cooperation can become a way of life. The second part of Hayek's argument on the matter of cooperation is related to his understanding of information. Every individual in a society possesses a personal supply of information which cannot be known in its entirety by anyone else. This is the concept of knowledge of time and place for which Hayek is well-known, at least among economists. The beauty of the catallaxy is that it utilizes, via the price system, these individual, dispersed stores of information. There is a notion of human dignity inherent in the concept of such individualized information which many critics fail to note. A system which provides the opportunity for each individual to use that knowledge for personal purposes respects individuality in a way command economies cannot.

Beside implying respect for individual dignity, does the catallaxy promise as many glorious benefits for individuals as it does for society as a whole? Here Hayek is admirably honest: while the catallaxy does provide people many of the "goodies" they want in life, it does so at a certain cost. The catallaxy does not supply individuals a moral vision of a good life to pursue; it does not guarantee happiness; it does not and cannot guarantee security.   In addition, it requires, as long as a few efficient individuals exist that all individuals must be efficient. They must consider the means they use in efforts to reach certain goals; in Hayek's terms, they must be responsible. Individual responsibility is one aspect of the discipline of the market.

To summarize: the value lying behind the third premise, then, is that the catallaxy accomplishes great good for mankind. Wealth, progress, and peaceful cooperation depend upon catallaxy. Because of this crucial connection between catallaxy and civilization, all institutions can be judged in terms of whether or not they are conducive to the catallaxy.

The theme of admiration for and appreciation of the catallaxy runs throughout Hayek's work. Is it also invoked to justify his constitutional design? In other words, does he become interested in constitutional engineering primarily in order to preserve the market, or to end interference with the market? My own perspective is that the market as such is not Hayek's end goal; the forces driving his venture into constitutional reform consist of a broader understanding of the prerequisites of ordered liberty. The market has a distinct role to play and makes its own indispensable contribution, according to Hayek, but it is one element in a broader constellation. That broader constellation of ordered liberty requires a "background of unwritten traditions and beliefs" (1979, p. 108) relating to law, justice, and the proper role of governments. It is this background, says Hayek, that "will have to be spelled out" if written constitutions are to protect ordered liberty.

It remains true that the catallaxy is important for ordered liberty. Two principles can be derived from Hayek's exploration of catallactic orders. The positive principle is that catallaxy should be used as much as is possible. As many activities as possible should be carried out in the market sphere. In his early work, Hayek referred to this as the principle of liberalism. The negative principle with which Hayek became more concerned in his later works, is that interference by means of specific commands must be avoided (1976, p. 128). Political actors are to dwell only upon improving the general rules of conduct on which the catallaxy rests.

Interference, in fact, creates privilege in the Great Society. Hayek's denunciation of governmentally conferred privilege is a reflection of his perceptions about justice in general. He does not commit himself to a defense of market justice. By market justice I mean a belief that the distributive results of market order are just. Distribution of goods, according to Hayek, is not a proper subject for assessments of or the content of our understanding of justice. The justly ordered society is one in which the particulars of any human wealth situation are not the topic of the laws of justice; instead justice relates to the equal application of the laws under which all individual behavior must be judged.

Yet Hayek's position is most often viewed as the equivalent of a defense of the status quo, and a status quo in which some benefit a great deal more than do others. A sophisticated and reasonable statement of this objection is given by Larry Preston, when he argues that the legitimacy of liberal society is made questionable by the perception that the market society selectively benefits "the most advantaged members of society" (1983, p. 673). Hayek, like other liberals, has responded with a "protracted effort to demonstrate the mutual benefits of strict adherence to liberal principles" (1983, p. 673). In less temperate and more impassioned form, Christian Bay raises the same issue. He argues that Hayek's statement of the truism that

"the enjoyment of personal success for large numbers
depends on rapid progress" (1971, p. 116) glosses over
the realities of market societies.

> Yet precisely this thin humanistic veneer is what
> makes Hayek's message such a welcome boost to the
> forces of greed and oppression: like a promise of
> pie in the sky, the promise of _eventual_ benefit to
> most of mankind provides a shallow justification,
> to many conservatives and liberals with shallow
> concerns for social or international justice, for
> continuing to enjoy the blessings and comforts of
> habitual middle-class liberties without guilty
> knowledge or a guilty conscience, or even much
> thought about the plight of others (1971, p. 116).

There are strong reasons issuing from Hayek's own
epistemology and views of cultural evolution to argue
against staking constitutional revolution on the need
to preserve an unhampered market. Perhaps this is why
he draws his case in considerably broader terms. For
the difficulty which is set up if reform or change is
to depend upon whether or not political institutions
interfere with the marketplace, is when does
interference become so unacceptable that the risk of
constitutional revolution is undertaken? A
considerable body of evidence from the second half of
the twentieth century indicates that catallactic orders
are remarkably resilient. While it is not clear how
much governmental "interference" a catallactic order
can absorb, it is clear that a wide variety of
interference (some indeed along lines justified by
Hayek in _The Constitution of Liberty_) has been absorbed
without destroying the order.
This observation is supported by viewing market
processes in terms of exchanges of information. Actors
in a market order must cope with constantly changing
information. Governmental interference is another
uncertain factor of production about which actors seek
information. At some point, obviously, if no
expectations can be formed about what government will
do (which some might say is a distinct possibility in
the not so distant future) individual planning will
become perilous.
Another way of viewing the matter of governmental
interference with the market order is in terms of
cultural evolution. From that perspective, a trial and
error process may be taking place in which "successful"
governmental intrusions into the marketplace will be
selected and retained. Some have even suggested that
such intervention may lengthen the lifespan of the
market, and secure a greater degree of harmony in
society at large that allows the market to function

(Buchanan 1977, Robbins 1963). What would Hayek regard as "successful," in addition to preserving the market order? To answer this question in any meaningful way beyond that of survival, we must turn to his definition of ordered liberty.

Hayek's call for reform of political institutions is not issued because the market order alone is threatened, but because interference in the market is symptomatic of the broader trend away from reliance on unpredictable individual planning toward constructivist rationalism. When government plans, even or perhaps especially, in pursuit of great achievements, take precedence over individual planning, then individual freedom may be imperiled.

NOTES

1.   On the general topic of "latent" functions dominating "manifest" functions of organizations, see Merton (1968), pp. 114-136; for a particular study on the same topic, see Selznick (1949).
2.   Change has obtained such an overwhelmingly positive connotation
      that we hardly note the implied value judgement in favor of change when it is discussed.
3.   For a similar argument cautioning against liberation for fulfillment of "natural" desires, see Campbell (1975).
4.   It is worth noting that once the notion of exchange is introduced, even when coercion is present, that the question of who benefits arises as a matter of justice. This is not the case where confiscation as a routine way of creating wealth prevails.

☆ 5 ☆

The Central Core:
The Proud and Comfortable
Sentiment of Liberty

I maintain that the premise which best appears to fit
the textual evidence of the span of Hayek's writings
from his earliest ventures into social philosophy into
his most recent explications of a constitutional order
is that his judgements of when respect and when
redesign for political institutions are required
revolve around his principle of ordered liberty.
Ordered liberty consists of the classical liberal
definition of liberty given shape by Hayek's emphasis
on the role played in human life by tacit knowledge and
evolved traditions. His presentation is and will, I
suspect, remain ambiguous, in large part because of his
emphasis on the importance of tacit knowledge.

Tacit knowledge provides the soil in which moral
principles take root and grow; Hayek is convinced that:

> the social world is governed in the long run by
> certain moral principles on which the people at
> large believe. The only moral principle which has
> ever made the growth of an advanced civilization
> possible was the principle of individual freedom,
> which means that the individual is guided in his
> decisions by rules of just conduct and not by
> specific commands (1979, p. 151).

Individual freedom, or what I term ordered liberty,
makes possible the development of a civilization in
which individuals are free to critically evaluate the
rules of just conduct by which they live. Without such
a civilization, liberty becomes meaningless; therefore
a commitment to ordered liberty implies a commitment to
the kind of civilization in which ordered liberty can
flourish. In Hayek's early work, this commitment
requires individual moral responsibility in general and
conscientious application of moral rules in particular
situations:

Freedom to order our own conduct in the sphere
where material circumstances force a choice upon
us, and responsibility for the arrangement of our
own life according to our own conscience, is the
air in which alone moral sense grows and in which
moral values are daily re-created in the free
decision of the individual (1944, p. 212).

It is only where the individual has choice, and
its inherent responsibility, that he has occasion
to affirm existing values, to contribute to their
further growth, and to earn moral merit...and in
doing so to create particular values (1967, p.
230).

It is in Hayek's later work that he minimizes the role
of the individual, and particularly individual reason,
and emphasizes the necessity of submission to tradition
in an unreflective way in order to preserve
civilization. This shift is occasioned in large part
by his own inability to accept a definition of ordered
liberty in which the elements of connectedness to one's
culture and traditional morality peacefully coexist
with critical exercise of one's individual reason.[1]
The shift contributes to the ambiguity of Hayek's work,
raising questions about whether his central commitment
is to civilization and progress or to the concept of
ordered liberty.

The ambiguity at the heart of his definition of
ordered liberty provides one of the major means to
refute my contention that the central principle in his
philosophy is ordered liberty rather than progress.
His idea of liberty is complex and unfamiliar, blending
as it does a set of factors which are in fundamental
opposition to one another. This complexity and its
ambiguity in Hayek's presentation do not disqualify it
as the guiding element in his philosophy. I believe
the full extent to which it is the driving force in
Hayek's work will appear in the pages to follow.

The other major way in which my position can be
refuted is more troubling. This is by focusing on the
tendency which has increased in intensity and emphasis
in Hayek's later work on the topic of cultural
evolution. The thrust of a great deal of that later
work is in the direction of skepticism about any human
capacity to shape the course of human events. Not only
does the rejection of constructivist rationalism
persist, but it is accompanied by what appears to be a
denunciation of reason in favor of blind faith. "Thus
the social order depends on a system of views and
opinions which we imbibe, inherit, and learn from a
tradition that we cannot modify" (1983, p. 56). This
echoes the earlier statement that what has made men

good is "neither nature nor reason but tradition" (1979, p. 160).

Yet in each case of denunciation of reason, it is implicitly affirmed within a few sentences that Hayek has not completely given up the possibility that human reason is sufficient at least to recognize the truth of his statements! In the former case, he adds: "I rather expect you to revolt against most of what I have said. I only hope that you will very seriously reflect upon it" (1983, p. 56); in the latter he notes, a bit further on, after noting that man's reason now makes him try to construct the order of society, that an important task of our intelligence is to "<u>discover</u> the significance of rules we never deliberately made" (1979, p. 163, emphasis added). His warning is not that we must give up reasoning or discovery, but that we must recognize the origins of and conditions for the exercise of reason. His despair about modern man's ability to acquire this perspective is what, I believe, drives him into his stance of blind faith in cultural evolution. The irony of this stance is that it results from a failure to develop the full implications of his own understanding of ordered liberty. By remaining anchored within the paradigm of the unencumbered self, Hayek cannot see a route by which modern individuals can embrace critical reason and cultural traditions simultaneously. Once we liberate his understanding from these shackles, and modify it with elements drawn from the situated self paradigm, a more optimistic outcome will ensue.

I turn now to Hayek's definition of ordered liberty. The definition of liberty with which he begins is a variant of "negative liberty." An individual is free in the sphere in which he or she can act without interference from other individuals. In any group of individuals, providing this freedom for more than one person requires that rules exist which guarantee to all individuals a sphere of action. In society, an individual is free when formal rules, known in advance, delineate these individual domains. In this account, the individual as unencumbered self predominates, a self pursuing self-interested goals within what are regarded, primarily, as constraints on individual freedom of choice.

Hayek does not remain unambiguously within the concept of the unencumbered self because he adds to the concept of negative liberty his understanding of man as a social animal. Historical, concrete human beings, about whom Hayek is concerned, are born into society. In this matter, individuals do <u>not</u> have a choice. Individuals may subsequently choose to attempt to break all social ties, or deny one societal affiliation in favor of another, but an individual remains a social

being.[2] This does not imply that the social context
necessarily will nourish rather than deny individual
freedom. While an individual can never be totally free
of a social context, there are different degrees of
liberation within society. With this background
established, there are two aspects of Hayek's
understanding I take particular care to set out: the
notion of limits, including his connection of liberty
to practical liberty, involving the necessity of
preserving life, and the idea of liberty as social in
character. In both these aspects, Hayek continues to
veer between the concepts of the unencumbered and
situated self. In the latter half of this chapter, I
seek to clarify Hayek's understanding of liberty in
relation to other contemporary liberal thinkers. First
I argue for a reinterpretation of Hayek's attack on
social justice as a critique of distinctly Rawlsian
nature. Then I apply the logic of Sandel's critique of
Rawls to Hayek. The unstated assumptions about and
understandings of the person, or self, employed by
Hayek emerge from this procedure. This supplies the
foundations for the assessment to be developed in the
final chapter of this work.

THE LIMITS AND DISCIPLINE OF LIBERTY: LIBERTY FOR LIFE

Hayek's concept of liberty has informed most of
his works in social and political thought. It is the
constant theme to which he returns again and again,
viewing it from many angles and turning it over and
over for consideration in his mind. The key to
understanding Hayek on liberty is to recognize that a
reflection on limits runs throughout his treatment.
This is a result of his conception of the individual
human being as imperfect and thus limited in what he or
she can accomplish. This does not mean individuals can
accomplish nothing; it does not imply a fatalistic
quietude toward the world. It represents a sober yet
matter-of-fact judgement about the limits of individual
action.

Hayek has no difficulties admitting these limits,
and they set the agenda of his political philosophy.
Individuals cannot do many things; they cannot create a
new world or change the human nature of their fellow
citizens. As we have noted already, human reason is a
great gift, but it too is limited. Accepting this,
Hayek can still reflect upon the ways in which reason
can be used, and with what consequences. In the same
way, Hayek begins from a notion that the freedom of an
individual is limited. He wants to discover how
individual reason can be used to further and protect
individual liberty. He sets out on this search without

any illusions that either reason or liberty can be made perfect or absolute. What are the possibilities for and limits of ordered liberty? Practically, Hayek argues, given man's social nature and social existence, the individual can be liberated from: (1) the dictated purposes of small, closed social groups such as the tribe, and (2) the dictates of a small political elite in an advanced society. At the same time, if individuals desire both survival and prosperity for large numbers of people (and Hayek assumes most people do) then, Hayek argues, the individual <u>cannot</u> be liberated from: (1) the discipline of nature and (2) the discipline of the market order.

The two types of centrally directed authority from which Hayek believes individuals can be liberated do not require much discussion here. To the extent that individuals voluntarily choose to become members of small groups and share the goals and follow the dictates of such a group, Hayek accepts small group dominion. Where this principle is transferred to the political sphere and made a coercive principle over a society as a whole, he believes freedom cannot flourish. Similarly, Hayek believes that the centrally planned society requires not only an elite but a requirement that all members make the aims of "the Plan" their own. In both cases, Hayek believes that not only is it essential for human dignity that individuals are allowed to pursue their own plans but that unless they can do so, a prosperous society will not result. Liberation of individuals in terms of liberation to devise their own plans can and must be defended as an essential element of individual liberty.

Liberation of individuals from nature and from the market cannot, Hayek believes, be defended if one values life, liberty, and prosperity. I juxtapose the "unfreedom" of man against nature and man against market because I think it reveals most clearly an element of Hayek's philosophy some readers miss. Hayek does not argue that the market is "natural" in the sense that a hurricane or volcanic eruption is a natural phenomenon. Yet the market does act upon individuals in unpredictable ways, as does nature. There is no manager of nature to whom one can complain; in a similar way, Hayek contends, there is no manager of the market. The market process, like nature, is a result of the actions of many unpredictable elements. To predict the results would require either that we were omniscient or that the elements involved behaved consistently. Neither natural elements nor individuals, however, behave with such consistency.

The market-nature analogy is useful for considering the different reactions of individuals to occurrences in each sphere. When a hurricane destroys a beach town, there is little attempt made to finger the source of blame, or the "exploiter" of the town's position. This sounds nonsensical. It has, apparently, become accepted that government (acting for the entire society, presumably) aids those whom nature has so unkindly treated. But this is not considered normally to be an issue of justice.

Within the market setting, the situation for affixing blame is much different. When a business which employed a considerable number of townspeople folds, or moves operations to a more profitable location, there is often a response phrased in terms of exploitation, or perhaps (not any less damning) the lack of a social conscience. Whether or not poor management, high wages, changing demand, or a changed environment have contributed to the decisions is not routinely discussed. A person or set of persons is to be identified as the source of the calamity. Yet the same individuals, when they began the business, may have received no particular commendations. Community leaders now apparently feel little remorse when they outbid a neighboring town and take hundreds of jobs out of that community's grasp. And individuals often leave important positions on short notice for the sake of monetary gain, and they are not considered, nor consider themselves to be, exploiters of the company whose employment they leave.

Often it seems that the benefits of the market (a wide variety of goods and services for the vast majority of people) in advanced societies are assumed to be natural, much as people assume the presence of natural resources like sunshine and rain. But in the latter case, cloudy days, drought, hail, and so forth, are routinely accepted as less desirable but still natural phenomena. Nature is a package deal: one cannot choose only the parts one prefers. The market must also be accepted as a package, in Hayek's view. The benefits accrue and so do the costs. Just as individuals do not think of themselves as less free because natural calamity may overtake them, so individuals cannot feel less free because the market may not meet their needs or their desire for security.

The market package Hayek advocates cannot and will not "free" man from society or the necessity of making a living. In fact, there is a subtle theme present in Hayek's treatment of the market which consists more of a lament than a celebration. He celebrates the creative energy of a market order relying upon individual actions, although without the eloquence of Marx. Where Marx wrote movingly of the plight of workers in factories, Hayek writes compellingly of the "burden of choice" an individual faces in a complex market society. Every human being, he notes, "is led

by the growth of civilization into a path that is not
of his own choosing." We are "not only the creatures
but the captives of progress" (1960, pp. 50, 52).

Modern man's "captivity," against which so many
individuals rebel, is painful precisely because there
is not a captor we can identify. I believe Hayek
identifies an important part of the "powerlessness"
which many people feel in a modern, capitalist society.
In such a specialized and complex society, the success
of individuals requires that they find the right use
for their particular abilities.

> As society and its complexity extend, the rewards
> a man can hope to earn come to depend more and
> more, not on the skill and capacity he may
> possess, but on their being put to the right use;
> and both the difficulty of discovering the best
> employment for one's capacities and the discrep-
> ancy between the rewards of men possessing the
> same technical skill or special ability will
> increase....The necessity of finding a sphere of
> usefulness, an appropriate job, ourselves is the
> hardest discipline that a free society imposes on
> us (1960, p. 80).

This discipline is resented, particularly by those who
understand liberty to mean that the individual should
be the master of his fate. (Socialist thinkers
recognize that such mastery has yet to be attained in
noncapitalist societies as well.)

The desire for control over one's fate, for "my
life and decisions to depend on myself, not on external
forces of whatever kind" (Berlin 1969, p. 166) is the
essence of "positive" liberty. As Isaiah Berlin notes
in his essay on liberty, positive liberty is concerned
more with having control of authority than curbing
authority (1969, p. 166). Hayek, in his rejection of
the notion of positive liberty, draws upon the idea of
the limits of individual liberation. Positive liberty,
in the sense of freeing individuals from the discipline
of the market as described above, would require either
an attempt to "dose progress" or a willingness to turn
occupational decisions over to a central authority. In
the former case, enormous presumptions are made about
man's ability to control progress; in the latter, the
result is clearly a diminution of freedom by any
definition.

Hayek's notion of the discipline of individual
freedom can be summed up in one short phrase: "Either
both the choice and the risk rest with the individual
or he is relieved of both" (1944, p. 126). The idea of
freedom as liberation from a complex society or from
the necessity of seeking strategies for survival is

illusory. Material progress has freed and can free many individuals from exhausting daily hardships but there are limits to freedom even in a complex, advanced society.

LIBERTY AS A SOCIAL PRODUCT

Hayek envisions liberty as an artifact of a civilized social existence for human beings. What consequences does this have for Hayek's conception of liberty? First of all, it means that he does not begin from a notion of an "abstract" individual or a "Crusoe model." Nor does he consider man behind some kind of veil (Rawls 1971) in order to consider what liberty or justice means. An individual born into society does not in the daily course of events consider how much freedom he or she will trade for some amount of security--the model of man with which James Buchanan, and other contractarians, appear to work (Buchanan 1977). A social individual begins with certain beliefs about freedom, obedience to law, and security which are culturally acquired. At any time, liberty is a socially defined phenomenon.

It is in this sense that Hayek's statement that liberty is an artifact of civilization (1979, p. 163; 1960, p. 54) is to be understood. Individual liberty did not exist in primitive times, at least not in a form which twentieth-century people would recognize as comparable to our broad range of concrete individual liberties. To develop an idea of presocial liberty, of Crusoe man, or man the rational maximizer existing independently of social meanings transmitted culturally, is to fail to see the extent to which protection of liberty requires an evolved social context which permits and nourishes individual liberty. Social liberty means first of all that we are looking at the liberty of individuals in the context of a liberating civilization.

In Hayek's understanding social liberty means, second, that individuals born in free societies have a certain unique relationship to the law, and this relationship itself must be nurtured if the social context is to protect and not destroy individual freedom. This requires a considerable amount of explanation. Perhaps the best place to begin is by viewing the law as an evolved, organic growth rather than simply as a positive outcome of legislation. While some commentators believe Hayek is an advocate of an evolutionary version of natural law (Gordon 1981), I do not think Hayek intends this. He sees law as part of the evolved structure of a society, a structure which may not be entirely enunciated. It is this structure of right and wrong, defining permissible and impermissible behavior, that is passed on to children by family and other institutions. When legislation continually reshapes basic parts of the law or makes their applications arbitrary rather than according to consistently defined criteria, then it becomes more difficult for the law to be taught and passed on as part of an individual's social learning.

Part of that social learning has involved explicit reference to the duty which will one day have to be assumed of passing on the moral principles one is being taught. Part of traditional learning, in other words, involved the understanding that the world of tradition must be revered and transmitted faithfully. With that world of tradition came a way of understanding the essential social fabric of individual lives.

Kitwood (1983) has enunciated in succinct fashion the extent to which we draw upon the work of a set of eminent liberal thinkers whose doctrines presupposed and drew upon a social fabric which was in existence in their life-times. This assumed background, however, has been transformed since individuals like Smith wrote. In Kitwood's words, "we confront established paradigms which do not seem to take our social nature into account" (p. 226). The model of economic man as rational maximizer is one example of an inheritance deprived of its social fabric. One consequence of these established paradigms is that we find it difficult to think about social or cultural context without imagining that the notion of "free will" is being attacked. As an Austrian economist who stresses the satisfaction of subjective values as the source of individual motivation, Hayek is freer to explore cultural contexts than many economists.

Hayek, it seems to me, approaches the understanding of cultural and social values as "constitutive" of an individual's identity found in the communitarian critique of liberalism as expressed in the work of Michael Sandel. In this sense, our understanding of law (and when it can be obeyed or disobeyed) becomes a part of our identity and influences how we think of freedom. Hayek certainly does not view freedom as something that atomistic individuals possess and which they may be willing to trade. Here we encounter one of the ways in which Hayek turns toward the concept of the situated self, a self for whom, in his account, the law and concept of freedom form a structure of identity prior to conscious rational choice.

The unique emphasis in Hayek's hesitant and fragmented picture of the situated self stems from the role played for such selves by the law. To the extent that a "community" can be identified in a Great

Society, membership in that community is at least partially dependent upon shared adherence to a particular tradition of law. A "public interest" or common interest exists: the continued preservation and development of that body of law which has defined the behavior condoned by the community. My main goal here is to establish that, for Hayek, freedom as social freedom is meaningless without awareness of the importance of law for the social context in which an individual may be free. It is for this reason that Hayek devotes so much time to his consideration of the "Rule of Law." We will return to this idea below.

PATTERNED JUSTICE: HAYEK AND RAWLS ON SOCIAL JUSTICE

Liberty as the Defense of Privilege?

A considerable part of the criticism of Hayek's concept of liberty is in fact directed toward his ideas of justice. I will explore one such perspective, in which Hayek is seen as a defender of a "negative liberty" which benefits only the wealthy, in order to introduce the variety of ways in which Hayek's views of justice are misunderstood. The proponent of this point of view on whom I will focus is Christian Bay. Bay's review, published in 1971, of The Constitution of Liberty conveniently summarizes many of the "progressive liberal" (in the sense of modern, rather than classical, liberal) arguments against Hayek's position.

The most serious objection Bay raises is that the discipline of the market falls more harshly on certain classes of people than on others. This is because market institutions, as well as the laws within which markets operate, reflect class interests (1971, p. 115). The interesting point, which Bay has missed, is that Hayek acknowledges (although not often nor with particular emphasis) that laws may in fact have been shaped with the interests of a particular class in mind. It remains the case that Hayek does not indicate that reform is indicated when such a situation has been identified; progressives may therefore snort at his simple observation, although the complexities of redressing past injustices must give anyone, progressive or conservative, pause. Hayek stresses throughout his writing that the rules governing market behavior can and must be improved upon. The criteria for such improvements are liberty and conduciveness to efficiency. This doctrine has a radical potential which liberals like Bay fail to comprehend.

Bay does us the service of presenting a sharply contrasting, positive definition of liberty. Hayek's definition, he warns, is so narrow as to include only "special liberties" appealing mainly to the rich. Bay's definition, he tells us, is for "the freedom of all men equally;" freedom is defined broadly, "to encompass, in principle all of man's most pressing needs, beginning with the need to stay alive" (1971, p. 121). This includes "freedom from the indignities of suddenly being left with no income, regardless of whether this happens on account of the arbitrary decision of an employer or whether one is victimized by technological change" (1971, p. 118).

The radically positive concept of liberty to which Bay adheres can be defended as exhibiting "a commitment to equalizing the worth of liberty" (Winston 1983, p. 331). But this commitment, when taken seriously, seems to require vast governmental action. A government would have to attempt, first, to provide a set of "basic goods" that would provide "minimum conditions" for living a life of independent choice. Winston lists such a set of basic goods, commenting that the legislation needed to realize these goods would be extensive (1983, p. 334). Second, a government would have to attempt to provide a freedom from risk for members of society, a task which is truly awesome. Such a provision could only be approximated through wide-ranging coercive direction of society. This possibility does not appear to bother Bay, who believes "rational planning" is the answer.

> Variety and experimentation are healthy in every society, and planners ought to study the free play of preferences in action....But the basic necessities of a decent life for all must come first, and that takes rational planning, with resources so large that only elected governments should be entrusted with them (1983, p. 119, emphasis added).

It seems only a short step from this position held by Bay to the argument that elected representatives or benevolent bureaucrats are better equipped to determine the "real" needs of the people than are the individuals themselves. The resemblances between this patronizing progressive statement and the aristocratic claim to know the people's interests better than they do themselves are striking. This argument can only be understood to deny the truth that each individual has a life and choices of his own (Berlin 1969, p. 127). Bay's concern for individual liberty seems to have no place for an understanding of liberty as a generator of progress as well as a source of dignity and individual responsibility in the face of different choices.

While Bay's critique is suffused with a

self-righteous "philosophical radicalism" that makes it difficult to treat seriously, the main issue should not escape us. It is, I believe, tied to the ideas of compassion and a sense of justice. "Respect for the principles of justice, or shame at gross inequality of treatment, is as basic in men as the desire for liberty" (Berlin 1969, p. 170). Liberals such as Bay are, I believe, genuinely disturbed by the existence of starving children, filthy housing, wretched living conditions, vast disparities of wealth, and limits to the control of the environment in which one must live. The question to which compassion directs us is--how can the situation be improved? To accuse Hayek of a total lack of compassion, as Bay does, is to willfully ignore the disciplined and somewhat sorrowful examination Hayek makes into the nature of governmentally-designed "compassion." The American experience with the Great Society should surely have persuaded us that a massive assault on inequality via coercive, centralized techniques has grave shortcomings and unexpected consequences.

Liberal frustration with Hayek centers on the fact that he neither has nor advocates immediate solutions for human suffering. In fact, Hayek <u>does</u> advocate establishing an income floor for those who have failed or have had bad luck in the market game. This could be done without necessitating a vast apparatus of central control. But he does not advocate any attempt to liberate people from the situation of risk and choice that defines their humanness even while it generates the material progress most individuals seem to desire.

This discussion of Bay's criticisms of Hayek draws attention to the uncomfortable and costly nature of freedom provided in Hayek's account. One of the most compelling features of his account is the honesty with which he presents his concept of liberty. Hayek's philosophy is firmly anchored in the world of scarcity, unpredictability, and bad luck. The freedom to succeed means also the freedom to fail, and neither alternative is a guarantee of happiness. In a time when a solution to every ill is thought to be just around the corner, Hayek reminds us that ordered liberty cannot "solve" lasting pains and dilemmas of human life.

Hayek and Rawls on the Sense of Justice

What role, then, does a basic sense of justice play in Hayek's philosophy? On the topic of justice, and particularly whether a sense of justice can be given in terms of distributive justice, the position of Hayek is nearly identical to that of John Rawls. If anything, Rawls appears to state even <u>more</u> clearly than does Hayek why "justice" as a concept cannot be said to apply to market-generated distributions. This convergence of views appears to account for Hayek's conclusion that he and Rawls agree "on what is to me the essential point" (1976, p. xiii). This point is that the principles of justice do not apply to distributions of desired things but "define the crucial constraints which institutions and joint activities must satisfy if persons engaging in them are to have no complaints against them" (from Rawls 1963, cited in Hayek 1976, p. 100).

Robert Nozick's discussion of "patterning" in terms of distributive justice provides an explanation for the striking similarities between the positions of Rawls and Hayek on patterned distribution in general and distribution according to moral merit in particular. Nozick's definition of patterned justice is as follows.

> Let us call a principle of distribution patterned if it specifies that a distribution is to vary along with some natural dimension, weighted sum of natural dimensions, or lexicographic ordering of natural dimensions. And let us say a distribution is patterned if it accords with some patterned principle....Almost every suggested principle of distributive justice is patterned: to each according to his moral merit, or needs, or marginal product, or how hard he tries, or the weighted sum of the foregoing, and so on (1974, pp. 156-157).

Nozick notes, as did Irving Kristol (1970) before him, that Hayek rejects any attempt to base distribution upon assessments of moral merit. But Nozick then attempts to argue that Hayek "himself suggests a pattern he thinks justifiable: distribution in accordance with the perceived benefits given to others" (1974, p. 158). While some of Hayek's comments do convey the impression that distribution reflects, to some extent, the benefits of one's services or goods for others, the whole of his treatment of the market mechanism issues in a far more complex understanding. Eamonn Butler summarizes Hayek's perception of market rewards as dependent upon "complex values and relationships between many suppliers and many buyers" (1983, p. 93). The particular pattern of distribution generated by market interactions at any one point in time is not a basis for judging the justice of a market society.

In A Theory of Justice, Rawls argues in a similar way that the proper topic for investigations into justice is the "background conditions," the

institutions and structures of a society, rather than
any particular distribution of benefits. His
conception of distributive justice "contains a large
element of pure procedural justice" (1971, p. 304).
What is important is to "set up and to administer
impartially a just system of surrounding institutions"
(1971, p. 304). He argues that the account of
distributive shares he supplies "is simply an
elaboration of the familiar idea that income and wages
will be just once a (workably) competitive price system
is properly organized and embedded in a just basic
structure" (1971, p. 304).

Rawls is sensitive to the contention that "men
cannot accept the historical accidents of the
marketplace--seen merely as accidents--as the basis for
an enduring and legitimate entitlement to power,
privilege, and property" (Kristol 1970, p. 9). Rawls
acknowledges that his version of justice as fairness in
this respect ill "accords with commonsense precepts of
justice" (1971, p. 304), but argues that commonsense
norms must be kept in a subordinate place. "None of
these precepts can be plausibly raised to a first
principle....Adopting one of them as a first principle
is sure to lead to the neglect of other things that
should be taken into account....what really counts is
the workings of the whole system and whether these
defects are compensated for elsewhere" (1971, pp.
307-309). Rawls goes on to suggest that the workings
of the market, taken in their totality, contradict a
variety of commonsense precepts. Again, he discounts
the importance of the discrepancy between commonsense
norms and his own principles. "It is more important
that a competitive scheme gives scope for the principle
of free association and individual choice of occupation
against a background of fair equality of opportunity,
and that it allows the decisions of households to
regulate the items to be produced for private purposes"
(1971, p. 310).

The fundamental similarity between Rawls and Hayek
on justice is that both reject the idea that a sense of
justice can only be satisfied by a pattern of
distribution. In one sense, their answer is the same
as that of Nozick, who asks: "must the look of justice
reside in a resulting pattern rather than in the
underlying generating principles?" (1974, p. 158-159)
Rawls's response is more radical than Hayek's in one
sense: he simply dismisses the commonsense morals which
Hayek believes have led to much of the demand for
social justice, and the dismissal is brusque. Despite
their prominence in our thinking, says Rawls, "[n]one
of these precepts can be plausibly raised to a first
principle" (1971, p. 307).

Rawls goes on, however, to identify a source of

the confusion about justice which Hayek has not
discussed. Rawls identifies the problem in a confusion
of commonly held views about retribution (as in
criminal law) and distribution. For while the view
that punishment for violation of laws indicates bad
character, or lack of moral character, has considerable
basis in a just society, the converse is not true.
"Even when things happen in the best way, there is
still no tendency for distribution and virtue to
coincide" (1971, p. 314).

Rawls offers two additional accounts of why people
tend to mistakenly identify distribution with virtue.
In both accounts, he and Hayek stand on virtually the
same ground. The first is that people fail to
understand the function of unequal shares of wealth.
That function, he says, "is to cover the costs of
training and education, to attract individuals to
places and associations where they are most needed from
a social point of view, and so on" (1971, p. 315).
Hayek explains the same function in different words
when he comments that it is "where most people do not
comprehend the usefulness of an activity" that "the
outcry about the injustice of it arises" (1976, p. 77).
"What those who attack great private wealth do not
understand is that it is neither by physical effort nor
by the mere act of saving and investing, but by
directing resources to the most productive uses that
wealth is chiefly created" (Hayek 1976, p. 98). This
follows from his general pessimism about the ability of
individuals to comprehend the workings of the abstract
principles of the market.

Rawls's second account bases the complaints about
the lack of social justice on what Hayek terms
"primordial" moral instincts. In an almost testy
fashion, Rawls rejects the notion that what people are
entitled to corresponds with their intrinsic moral
worth. I quote at length from Rawls here, because I do
not believe it is widely recognized that some of the
positions on social justice found so reactionary in
Hayek are also to be found in Rawls.

> Surely a person's moral worth does not vary
> according to how many offer similar skills, or
> happen to want what he can produce. No one
> supposes that when someone's abilities are less in
> demand or have deteriorated (as in the case of
> singers) his moral deservingness undergoes a
> similar shift. All of this is perfectly obvious
> and has long been agreed to. It simply reflects
> the fact noted before that it is one of the fixed
> points of our moral judgments that no one deserves
> his place in the distribution of natural assets
> any more than he deserves his initial starting

place in society (1971, p. 311).

Moral worth is not what the market measures. And
therefore in a market society, both Hayek and Rawls
maintain that what matters is procedural justice,
rather than any particular pattern which may result
from market interactions, and that efforts to create a
just distribution are both impractical and ill-advised.
    This account of the similarities between Hayek and
Rawls on the matter of distributive justice is designed
only for the limited purpose of illuminating Hayek's
concept of liberty. It is not intended to advance the
argument that Hayek and Rawls develop similar theories
of justice. The fundamentally constructivist nature of
Rawls' work (which he emphasizes in the 1980 Dewey
lectures) alone sets him quite apart from Hayek, and
there are numerous other substantial differences.
However, both agree that justice is properly considered
in terms of background institutions of a society rather
than in terms of distribution of wealth.
    The proper assessment of justice forms a backdrop
to understanding Hayek's view of liberty. The freedoms
of choice of association and of occupation which
constitute a large part of Hayek's understanding of
liberty are not to be confused with either the
arbitrary facts of initial distributions of skill and
strength, or the processes by which the market directs
"ability to where it best furthers the common interest"
(Rawls 1971, p. 311). It is because in the market "we
all constantly receive benefits which we have not
deserved in any moral sense that we are under an
obligation also to accept equally undeserved
diminutions of our incomes...nobody [in the market] is
under an obligation to supply us with a particular
income [although we may choose, outside the market, to
supply a floor of income for all]" (Hayek 1976, p. 94).
Freedom implies responsibility as well as the bleak
fact that our choices will not work out as we had
hoped. The cry for social justice, Hayek argues, in a
way analagous to Rawls's comments on the basic aversion
to the arbitrary distribution of talents, arises out of
the childlike frustration that the world does not work
as we might like it to. Implicit in our complaints
against the justice of the market and our demands for
social justice is our resentment "that we tolerate a
system in which each is allowed to choose his
occupation and therefore nobody can have the power and
the duty to see that the results correspond to our
wishes" (1976, p. 69).

APPLYING SANDEL'S CRITIQUE OF THE UNENCUMBERED SELF

A second source of controversy in Hayek's work has revolved around a discussion of the extent to which Hayek's notion of the rule of law protects individual freedom. A rather large number of commentators appear to be in agreement that the rule of law cannot protect individual liberty without a notion of individual rights (Watkins 1961; Robbins 1963; Rees 1963; Hamowy 1971, 1978; Bay 1971; McClain 1979; Barry 1981). The argument, briefly, is that even if a law meets Hayek's tests of generality and equality, it may violate individual liberty.[3] A law requiring all individuals to worship Allah, for instance, could be general, abstract, and equally enforced but still would be an infringement on individual liberty.

Hayek himself has addressed the critics on this point (1973). The subject of rules of conduct, he maintains, is not what a person may or may not do within the privacy of his home, but an individual's conduct toward other persons. Rules of conduct instead delimit a "protected domain of individuals" (1973, p. 101). Hayek has at least superficially clarified his position on this criticism, although he has not attempted to specify the content or extent of the protected domain. This reveals the wide gap between Hayek's approach and theorists who begin from a concept of individual rights. Most of the critics cited above go on to make the case that Hayek's arguments would rest on firmer ground if he did have a theory of individual rights.

Why is there no attention to individual rights as such in Hayek? The treatment of liberty provided in this chapter supplies much of the answer. For Hayek, liberty is not an absolute or natural right; it represents rather the historical product of many hard-fought battles to limit the authority of government. Individual liberties, concrete liberties, did not exist in a presocial time; they have grown and been protected in civilized societies. Their continued protection requires stating them as principles, and willingness to sacrifice other goods for them, but Hayek does not rely upon any set of God-given or naturally existing rights. This, in my opinion, does not detract from Hayek's arguments in defense of liberty. As Cheyney Ryan has observed, "The problem with arguments which must assume a set of rights to make their appeals to personal liberty stick is that they will be of little consequence when confronted with views which reject their particular set of rights" (Ryan 1976, p. 141). Hayek also seems implicitly aware of the way in which an argument built upon rights can quickly be transformed into a positive conception of freedom such as that held by Bay. This reluctance to endorse an abstract set of rights seems consistent with Hayek's understanding of social liberty as well as his evolutionary approach.

There is, however, in Hayek's treatment of individual rights and the rule of law a disconcerting element. Hayek seems to assume that custom and tradition in Western civilization have defended and will defend the notion of the protected domain of the individual. By assuming that this domain is a "given," Hayek seems to ignore the fact that one of the topics of political debate is precisely where the line between public and private domains should be drawn. Once again we see that Hayek slips into treating "tradition" as an autonomous force, while in fact the evolving content of a "tradition" concerning individual liberty is the crucial issue. Given this domain, liberty requires the reduction of government coercion to the amount necessary to enforce rules of just conduct between individuals. This requirement is supplied by law meeting Hayek's criteria for the Rule of Law. Yet exactly how is the protected domain defined and protected?

Hayek fears that the protected domain of liberal and individualistic societies is withering away. In one sense, the body of his work can be interpreted as an effort to gain the attention of a populace (of intellectuals, at least) who do not see that their protected domains of liberty are slipping away. Indeed, the situation is so desperate, that Hayek suddenly and inconsistently calls upon those whom he has labored to teach of the value of rule following (and indeed, often unreflective rule following), to recognize the urgency of the situation and seek through rational constructivism to remedy the situation at hand.

It is here that the logic of Michael Sandel's critique of Rawls can be applied to Hayek's work as well. Sandel suggests that Rawls focuses upon the difficulty of justifying distributions of wealth which are fundamentally arbitrary--undeserving, as we have seen, in any moral sense. Most can agree that individual talents and assets are randomly distributed, according to natural abilities or inherited fortune. Rawls's principles of justice, however, according to Sandel, substitute one arbitrary situation for another. Behind the veil of ignorance, a principle of sharing is selected to guide distributive justice. Rawls fails to show us why rational individuals in the original position would embrace a principle of sharing such as is found in the difference principle. The ties of moral community, Sandel suggests, which one could argue would indeed found and ground such a principle of

sharing are explicitly denied to the individuals in the
original position.

What I argue here is that Hayek makes a similar
kind of mistake as does Rawls from a Sandelian
perspective. What would make his call for rational
defense of ordered liberty nonarbitrary and consistent
is an appeal to a preexisting understanding that all
members of a community must make judgements about their
shared objectives and institutions. But in Hayek's
account, such judgements are made by long-term
processes of cultural evolution rather than by
individuals.

The problem in Hayek's work, I believe, is rooted
in his flawed concept of liberty. He is so obsessed
with the belief that market constraints are the best of
all possible constraints (because they open up the most
options for individual choice) that he fails altogether
to see that an element of freedom resides in the choice
by individuals of constraints. His preoccupied focus
on market constraints may lead him to overvalue the
kind of choice making which the market system requires,
in addition to oversimplifying how market choices are
made. This kind of choice making, he suggests, is
primarily in the form of "rule following," with the
rules supplied by tacit knowledge which itself is
distilled from centuries of traditional knowledge of
"how" to do things. But in order for an individual to
make use of these kinds of rules successfully, is
simple following of formulaic rules enough?

In his zeal to caution against overestimation of
human reason, Hayek seems to lose sight of the role
which individual judgements must play even in everyday
market situations. The ingredients for success in the
marketplace, I argue, are in fact similar to the
ingredients needed for success in other kinds of
judgements. Hayek writes as if the unencumbered self
strolls blithely through the marketplace responding to
incontestable directives from an inner store of tacit
knowledge, uniquely his or her own. No one choice, I
would contend, is presented by general rules for
choice. Some alternatives can be eliminated,
certainly, but without, alas, narrowing the focus to
one optimal choice.

The overriding emphasis on blind rule following in
Hayek's work deprives him of recognizing the
interaction between judgement and rules that occurs
when people make choices. This may be due to his view
that particularistic, localized, or as he calls them
"tribal" ethics (which involve the serving of known
needs of known people) must routinely and
unreflectively be suspended in favor of universalized,
generalized, Great Society ethics, in which everyone is
treated as a moral equal so long as they are

participants in the marketplace who observe the market
rules. In effect, Hayek appears to deny to the
individual a capacity for moral judgement of any kind
so long as they remain within "market" settings.
Because he sees the coordination of the market as
crucial for the survival of large populations in
advanced industrial societies, he appears to accept
that individuals have to give up making judgements
related to "virtuous" behavior in large portions of
their lives. All that can be assessed, because of our
limited knowledge and our inability to predict
consequences of individual behavior in the aggregate,
is how well others follow the rules of the market. As
I indicated earlier, even this level of assessment is
fraught with ambiguity given the nature of the
catallaxy.

Leaving aside the difficulties of ascertaining who
observes the rules of the market, let us look at the
bind in which this overwhelming focus of Hayek's places
him. It is as though he advocates blind rule following
as a way of life, and suddenly in midstream says, but
not now. Why, will innocent converts inquire, should
they suddenly give up the principle which has made the
accomplishments of the Great Society possible? All
Hayek can rather lamely respond is that an
extraordinary threat to the civilization of the Great
Society (the encroachment on individual domains of
liberty) requires that the routine following of market
rules is no longer enough. Now individuals must step
out of their character as market participants and make
moral choices. Yet in terms both of practice in making
moral choices, as well as awareness of commonly held
values or goals which form some kind of reference point
for making such choices, the market society as Hayek
has defined it, denies to the members of the Great
Society the very qualities which are now required.

As I will argue in the next chapter, the flaw in
his concept of liberty revolves around his inability to
conceive of the essential role played by the moral
capacity for "judgement" in free individuals. A
complete account of tacit knowledge would include the
knowledge of one's social and moral bonds which each
person attains in some form in the earliest years of
life. What is required in the market society is not
the suppression of particularistic morals, which are
anchored in the social character of this part of tacit
knowledge, but the frequent and difficult exercise of
judgement, of knowing how "to select among the relevant
stack of maxims and how to apply them in particular
situations" (MacIntyre 1984, p. 223). Members of
market societies must make painful choices between
universalistic ethics and particularistic ethics,
ethics which are often in conflict. In effect,

individuals as they exercise judgement are selecting
which set of constraints is to guide their choice of
action in a particular situation.

If Hayek were able to see this and incorporate it
into his theory, a stronger definition of liberty would
result, and several inconsistencies would be cleared
up.   If individuals were regarded as people making
judgements, then Hayek's call for rational construction
of political institutions would be an appeal to shift
the direction of our judgements, rather than to
initiate a sudden change in behavior. In addition, we
would be able to understand that it is as many
individuals make constant evaluations of rules of
traditions, and when and how to apply them, that
traditions themselves evolve.   Otherwise, if
individuals are primarily and overwhelmingly rule
followers, we have considerable difficulty envisioning
how evolutionary change in traditions takes place. In
addition, regarding judgements between traditions and
rules in this way allows us to see that the "rules" of
the market society cannot be strictly identified--but
are a constantly changing set of codes of behavior all
of which together produce the kind of market society we
find at any given time. Individual liberty, as I will
argue in the next chapter, emerges when people
self-consciously evaluate the codes of behavior they
inherit in order to decide when, and whether, it is
appropriate to follow those codes as individuals and as
members of a community.

NOTES

1.   Hayek does, even in his early work, worry that
      "the consciousness that it is our individual duty
      to know how to choose" (1944, p. 212) has been
      eroded.   I suspect that Hayek may at some point
      have recognized that the virtuous individualist
      society he lauded was a figment of his imagination
      rather than an image based on some reality.
      Surely it is hard to believe a society exhibiting
      all the following virtues has ever existed:
      "independence and self-reliance, individual
      initiative and local responsibility, the
      successful reliance on voluntary activity,
      noninterference with one's neighbor and tolerance
      of the different and queer, respect for custom and
      tradition, and a healthy suspicion of power and
      authority" (1944, p. 215).
2.   Here Hayek and Marx seem to stand in agreement:
      "The individual is the social being. His life,
      even if it may not appear in the direct form of a
      communal life carried out together with others--is

therefore an expression and confirmation of <u>social life</u>" (Tucker 1978, p. 86).

3. The best account of this controversy, including his now revised and sympathetic position, is found in Gray 1986, pp. 62-68. He argues there that this criticism "seems to me to express an impoverished and mistaken view of the nature and role of Kantian universalizability in Hayek's philosophical jurisprudence" (p. 62).

☆ 6 ☆
Assessing Hayek's
Philosophy of Liberty

In this chapter I specify the unique contributions Hayek makes toward a philosophy of liberty first by assessing him in terms of the ideas of conservatism he molds into his liberal theory. Then I address how his vision of ordered liberty treats the theme of community, broadly defined. The similarities and differences between his vision and that of the communitarian critics of liberalism are discussed with particular attention to the work of Alasdair MacIntyre. In my concluding pages, I propose a new definition of liberty for the individual which goes beyond that of Hayek because it moves out of the paradigm of the unencumbered self and takes some steps in the direction of understanding implied by the idea of the "situated self."

HAYEK'S CONSERVATISM

The effort to assess what conservative insights Hayek brings to liberalism appears, at first glance, to be misguided. Hayek concludes his highly regarded tome, The Constitution of Liberty, with a postscript entitled, "Why I am Not a Conservative." In a generally unflattering portrait of conservatives, he attempts to distinguish himself from conservative thinkers. In somewhat oversimplified form, his criticism of conservatives is that their ideas reveal an absence of courage, fear of change, complacency about authority, and willingness to coerce in the name of ideals. On all these counts, Hayek says, he cannot be regarded as a conservative.

In this work in 1960, Hayek defends himself, and liberals, in ways which are eclipsed in his later works on the cultural evolution of humankind. Here, however, he claims that the liberal position "is based on

courage and confidence, on a preparedness to let change
run its course even if we cannot predict where it will
lead" (1960, p. 400).   That he feels "reverence for
some of the traditions" of his society, and that he is
willing to "seek assistance from whatever nonrational
institutions or habits have proved their worth," does
not prevent him from advocating "guiding principles
which can influence long-range developments" (1960, pp.
406, 408).

Setting aside terminological difficulties and the
later developments of Hayek's work for the moment, does
the bulk of Hayek's work fall within what are widely
regarded as central tenets of conservative thought?   In
a recent discussion of what such central tenets might
be, Linda Medcalf and Kenneth Dolbeare (1985) suggest
that at least five elements of what they term
traditional conservatism (or organic conservatism) can
be identified.   These are: (1) an emphasis on society
and its civilization rather than on the individuals who
make it up;   (2) a view of individuals as temporary
beneficiaries of society who have obligations to
contribute to society;   (3) the idea that traditional
moral values give life meaning;   (4) the concept that
change should be made in accordance with traditions and
the experience of a society;   and (5) the view of
society as an organic social whole with everyone in a
divinely ordained place.

To what extent does this summary also appear to
summarize Hayek's philsophy of liberty?   It is clear, I
believe, that Hayek (like Mill) considers individuals
and society as inextricably intertwined, and therefore
when he speaks of what is best for individuals he is
often in the same breath discussing how they contribute
the most to society.   The best examples of this can be
found in his discussions of the market, beginning from
early references and extending throughout his work.

> Our civilization advances by making the fullest
> use of the infinite variety of the individuals of
> the human species....Culture has provided a great
> variety of cultural niches in which that great
> diversity of men's innate or acquired gifts can be
> used.   And if we are to make use of the distinct
> factual knowledge of the individuals inhabiting
> different locations on this world, we must allow
> them to be told by the impersonal signals of the
> market how they had best use them in their own as
> well as in the general interest (1979, pp.
> 172-173).

The market, indeed, while it allows the individual to
harness his own knowledge of time and place, is valued
precisely because it is the mechanism which has made a

free civilization possible.

The theme of obligation to society runs throughout his work as well, although appearing in somewhat heavier form in his later work. As individuals, we only have a claim to society when we follow its rules; the benefits of civilization cannot be granted to all, disregarding whether or not they uphold the rules of that civilization. There is some ambivalence in Hayek's writings on this subject, in which he appears to defend applying some of the doctrines he explicitly connects to the closed or tribal society in the open society of Western civilization. I believe the ambivalence stems from the central role attributed to submission <u>without understanding</u> in Hayek's accounts of human society. For while individuals in the open society are freed from obedience to "compulsory common concrete purposes" (1983, p. 30) characteristic of tribal society, we remain subject to forces we cannot understand. "We stand in an enormous framework into which we fit ourselves by obeying certain rules of conduct that we have never made and never understood, but which have their reason" (1983, p. 46). To be part of any human society in Hayek's account, individuals must accept the authority of that society. In a very conservative stance indeed, Hayek affirms that "[w]hat makes an individual a member of society and gives him claims is that he obeys its rules" (1979, p. 172).

Hayek as a moral philosopher is resolutely quiet on the topic, "what is the meaning of life?" His early emphasis on human development and the exercise of one's intellect, appears to wind down into some rather general and vague affirmation of "the unfolding of the new." It could be noted, in his defense, that meaning is regarded always as an individual matter, and one of the chief benefits of the market order, according to Hayek, is that it allows people to pursue any number of final ends.

It is equally clear, however, that Hayek defends a way of life. Norman Barry (1984) suggests that this defense ultimately rests on quasi-utilitarian, consequentialist grounds alone. There is an alternative, however, which is to suggest that for Hayek the only meaningful way of life is that of freedom. This is not only because it will bring the benefits (materially speaking) of civilization, but because without freedom, there can be no morality. "That freedom is the matrix required for the growth of moral values--indeed not merely one value among many but the source of all values--is almost self-evident. It is only where the individual has choice, and its inherent responsibility, that he has occasion to affirm existing values, to contribute to their further growth, and to earn moral merit" (1978, p. 230). Freedom,

indeed, "requires not only strong moral standards but
moral standards of a particular kind....the values we
hold are the product of freedom....only societies which
hold moral values essentially similar to our own have
survived as free societies, while in others freedom has
perished" (1978, p. 230).

On the notion that change should be made in
accordance with traditions and experience, it could be
argued that the part of Hayek's attack on
constructivist rationalism dealing with the
substitution of individual rational design, or the
flights of fanciful reason, for the insights of
experience (leaving aside how one comes to assess and
know these insights) is indeed thoroughly conservative.
On the other hand, his willingness to reconstruct a
society in a piecemeal fashion, is far less
conservative. As I have shown, Hayek remains a liberal
in the sense that he is a meliorist, that, as he puts
it, "there has never been a time when...liberalism did
not look forward to further improvement of
institutions" (1960, p. 399).

Is it possible to interpret Hayek as viewing
society as divinely ordained in some fashion? Here I
think it is simply not possible to convincingly support
such an interpretation. There are occasionally
overtones in Hayek's work which seem to indicate some
belief in a direction for progress, or evolution, which
one might want to construe as a veiled belief in a
divinely ordained world in the process of becoming, but
it requires considerable imagination to adhere to such
an interpretation.

Hayek and Contemporary Conservatives

Given these clearly conservative elements in
Hayek's thought, it seems useful to examine what place
he holds in contemporary conservativism. This is
awkward, for just as Hayek himself has pointedly
disavowed the label of conservative, so have some
conservatives been more inclined to disclaim than claim
him as one of their own. Yet the image of Hayek as a
conservative persists. One reason for this seems to
lie in the middle ground Hayek occupies between (on the
libertarian left) Murray Rothbard and (on the right) a
more "European" conservative such as Russell Kirk. In
this section I will explore to what extent Hayek's work
represents a reconciliation of these two points of
view, and what this position reveals about his understanding of liberty.

Rothbard's concept of freedom is tied to notions
of moral rights and property. Freedom is the "absence
of invasion by another of anyone's person or property"

or natural moral rights (1982, p. 41). Natural
(legitimate) ownership of property occurs through the
use and transformation of nature-given resources (a
position drawing upon that of Locke and similar to that
of Nozick). A society of voluntary exchange consists
of exchanges of title to property. Such a society,
according to Rothbard, can achieve freedom and
abundance. There is no need for government in such a
society: government is illegitimate by definition,
since it exists only by invading the property of
citizens through taxation.

Hayek views the anarchist approach held by
Rothbard as inimical to human civilization, which
relies upon ties of cooperation between individuals
supported by a government of law. If all individuals
did the "right" things, anarchy might be a desirable
state. But as Norman Barry notes, "all would be well
if people followed natural law but the problem is that
diagnosed by Hobbes--however well-disposed each person
might be, fear and uncertainty about the behavior of
others drives people to form states" (Barry 1982, p.
120). For anarchists who defend anarchy even if people
are not good, and accept that the strong should subdue
the weak, Hayek has little patience. "With that type
of anarchism, I find it very difficult to sympathize.
I firmly believe, as I said before, that this sort of
anarchism would not produce anything called
civilization" (Hayek 1975, p. 10).

Despite this major difference between Rothbard and
Hayek on the legitimacy of government, the two thinkers
share a commitment to the centrality of the individual.
This individual in both theories is a productive,
materialist individual who acquires and values
property. To the extent that government interferes
with this individual pursuing the gainful use of
property, government violates freedom.

Hayek and Rothbard also share a perception of the
contrast between exchange and government as
coordinating mechanisms of individuals. However, Hayek
qualifies his argument in ways Rothbard does not.
Exchange is good when it occurs within a structure of
rules, and government is the necessary enforcer of
those rules. Government may but does not always invade
individual rights. Hayek's emphases are tempered
variants of libertarianism, and they are tempered by an
emphasis on order found in extreme form in Kirk.

Russell Kirk believes that "order is the first
need of the commonwealth," (1974, p. 6) and that
"authority is necessary for any truly human existence"
(1969, p. 285). Order as the first virtue of a society
may require the subordination of the individual to the
organic society of which he is but a part. Kirk, in
contrast to Rothbard, is interested in restraining the

materialist individual, largely through a return to a
moral society.   In his apocalyptic terms, Kirk
advocates understanding conservative ideals "so that we
may rake from the ashes what scorched fragments of
civilization escape the conflagration of unchecked will
and appetite" (1953, p. 10).

Kirk, in his devotion to a moral and hierarchical
order, accomplishes three things.   First, he cuts
himself off from the Western tradition of dynamic
change and dedication to material gain (O'Sullivan
1976, p. 148). Second, he denies that individuals have
a natural right to exercise political power.   Kirk
notes that "men do possess a natural right to be
restrained from meddling with political authority in a
fashion for which they are unqualified and which can
bring them nothing but harm" (1953, p. 53).   The
remarkable quality of this statement, it seems to me,
is that Kirk can so blithely ignore a whole chapter of
Western history surrounding the rise of the democratic
state.   Kirk's third accomplishment is to give the
appearance of rejecting reason in favor of veneration
of tradition, and freedom in favor of the custom-ruled
community.   In this way, order will be preserved and
individuals will be virtuous.

Hayek, like Kirk, values order and respects custom
and tradition.   Yet Hayek seems to speak to the
twentieth century in ways Kirk cannot. He acknowledges
that democracy must be regarded as the only viable rule
in the Western world; the challenge is not to push
democracy off the stage but to make it conducive to
individual liberty.   Hayek does not share Kirk's
longing for the community defined only by custom. Such
a community denies individuals the free use of their
reason and the full expression of their personality.

The emphasis shift from Rothbard to Kirk is from
the individual and liberty to society and order.   In
Hayek's philosophy, there is an attempt to provide for
both liberty and order, the individual and society.
Hayek's contention is that individual liberty is
fullest, most valuable for individual development, and
most useful in an ordered society.   In other words,
"the problem of political theory and political practice
is to bring about such conditions of order as make
possible the greatest exercise of freedom by the
individual" (Meyer 1962, p. 59).   This is the central
problem which has occupied Hayek.

Does the identification of conservative themes in
Hayek pursued above indicate to us the unique and
important contributions Hayek has made to liberalism
and the philosophy of liberty? So far, it seems to me
that we have learned very little.   The intricate
relationship between the individual and the society,
and the extent to which the liberty of the former

contributes to the latter, has been addressed by other
liberals, notably John S. Mill.   Is there more to be
learned?

John Gray believes there is. He suggests in fact
that Hayek brings a rich new strain to liberal thought
in his borrowings from conservatism. Referring to "one
of the most centrally important arguments" in Hayek's
work, Gray argues the following.

> I refer to his claim that human individuality
> depends for its exercise and even its existence on
> a cultural matrix of traditional practices which
> shape and permeate the moral and intellectual
> capacities of the individual....In making this
> claim, Hayek is synthesizing the insights of
> conservative philosophy...with the central
> concerns of classical liberalism....[H]is crucial
> distinction [is] between true and false
> individualism--between the individualism which
> sets man apart from society and the liberalism
> which sees man's individuality as an organic part
> of social life.   The key element is the
> distinction he finds in the different role
> allotted within each individualist tradition to
> the use of reason.   In the one, reason has an
> architectonic and constructive role, whereas in
> the other it is critical, exploratory and only one
> aspect of the process of cultural evolution (1986,
> p. 130).

I agree with Gray that this argument is crucially
important in Hayek's work, but in order to understand
it fully--and to fully assess his philosophy of
liberty--it is useful to recast Gray's insight by
seeing Hayek groping for an acceptable version of a
liberal community. While he does not succeed in the
positive task of creating such a vision, he does help
us to see that most modern and contemporary accounts of
community are fundamentally incompatible with ordered
liberty.

THE LIMITS OF COMMUNITY

Does Hayek's constitutional society of ordered
liberty in which individuals respond to market signals
negate the possibility of the realization of
"community"? Hayek is aware of the attractiveness of
the notion of "community" to many individuals in
advanced industrial societies. As Geraint Parry has
noted, the term "community" is rarely used in modern
social science literature in anything resembling a
negative context (Parry 1982). I argue here that

Hayek's vision of a free society resting on spontaneous evolutionary processes does contain a place for a limited sense of community.

It is true that any notion of a community based entirely on shared, concrete goals is precluded in the free society Hayek describes. The rise of the market society rests in part on the liberation of individuals from collective purposes. Freed from the requirement of working for objects dictated by the necessity of the community, the individual can pursue his or her own goals. Constraints on method of pursuit remain, of course; but the freedom to choose one's own purposes represents a substantial increase of individual liberty.

This increase of liberty means at the same time an increase in responsibility and autonomy, both of which can be painful conditions. The obedience to abstract rules demanded by the market has other, often unpleasant, consequences of which Hayek is aware. In the abstract market society, "wanting to do good to known people will not achieve the most for the community" (1979, p. 168). Does Hayek mean, then, that "doing good" has no place in advanced society? While his account tends to leave this impression, I do not think this is his intention. In fact, Hayek is arguing that a large society's activities can not be organized solely along the principle of "doing good" to individuals one knows. Such a principle cannot coordinate activities as does the price mechanism. Hayek perhaps fails to draw out clearly that it is the tension between wanting to do good and the necessities of responding to market signals that makes the idea of community solidarity so attractive. It is hoped that membership in a community can somehow alleviate this tension.

Hayek properly rejects the effort to prevent this tension by "free identification" of the individual with the aims of the state or collectivity. In this situation, civil society is "transcended," and a "higher" state of existence is reached. This appears to be the notion of organic community present in Hegel's understanding of the transcendence of civil society (for discussion, see Vernon 1976).

Another account of such a transcendence is found in Rousseau. An individual becomes fully free when all his needs can be met through participation in the community. Rousseau demanded from society

> more than the conditions for a moral life, more than the opportunity for self-development, more than material necessities. The community must be designed to satisfy man's feelings, to fulfill his emotional needs (Wolin 1969, p. 371).[1]

Such a total fulfillment of individual needs could result only from a feeling of solidarity generated from the pursuit of common ends on a statewide scale. Hayek's point is that any approximation of such a state would require either a complete change in human nature (by which a transcending of the market society would occur) or the end of what we think of as individuality, or massive coercion. The costs of these possibilities in terms of individual liberty as we know it are staggering.

More recent accounts of the potential for community have turned away from such total identification with the ends of the collectivity. One of the well-known advocates of community on a smaller scale, Michael Taylor, explicitly rejects the kind of transcendence discussed above. Community, he contends, need not require a "condition of 'transcendence' combined with a sense of belonging and mutual affirmation" (1982, p. 32). Taylor's vision is of a set of communities where problems of social control are solved without resorting to state coercion. For social control of this sort to be viable, several core elements of a community must be present. These include smallness of size, stability of population, and a "rough" economic equality. These factors facilitate a set of common beliefs and values, relations between individuals which are "direct and many-sided," and the practice of reciprocity.

What are the advantages Taylor sees in such a community? He seems to believe that coercion will be decreased because of the absence of the state, and that individuals will participate more directly in various forms of social control such as expressions of approval and disapproval through "gossip, ridicule, and shaming" (1982, p. 93). Would individual liberty decline in such a community? Taylor's answer is an ambiguous version of "not necessarily." Privacy, he admits, is not granted in very large amounts in such a community. This poses no real problem, however, for "privacy is in itself not a form of liberty" (1982, p. 159). Taylor also notes that for members of primitive and peasant communities, autonomy is not a problem (1982, p. 161). Taylor believes, however, that in "true" communities, which he suggests "secular family communes" approach, conditions would be conducive to the achievement of autonomy of action. I did not find Taylor's suppositions on this matter at all convincing.

Taylor's presentation represents another attempt to "solve" the tensions of autonomy an advanced market society brings to individuals. I find it difficult, however, to contemplate the solution he proposes. Does Taylor really think a return to shaming, ridicule, and gossip as forms of social control is acceptable in

return for the benefits of community? Contemplating
this possibility, one is tempted to share Hayek's bleak
prognosis that there is "very little hope" for
preserving the levels of civilization which we have
achieved (1979a, p. 10). The tensions of autonomy may
be one part of life in an advanced industrial society.

Hayek points to another difficulty of visions such
as Taylor's. Even setting aside the question of the
kind of individual liberty such communities would
provide, another problem emerges: how are economic
relations between communities to be ordered? Taylor
has admitted that he has found no solution to the
problem of relations-in-general between communities (in
the absence of the state). He assumes, for reasons not
clear to me, that because the communities would be
stateless as well as small, "the potential for
inter-communal aggression and exploitation would be
limited" (1982, p. 168). Even if aggression would
disappear with "the state" (as in the Marxist utopia?),
how would economic transactions between communities be
ordered? Taylor does not address this question.
Reliance on the market mechanism would seem to conflict
with the identified prerequisites for social control
without the state in such communities. Individuals
responding to market signals may violate the conditions
of stability, equality, and direct relations Taylor
discusses. Are the communities to be self-sufficient?

I suspect that Taylor's thinking about communities
rests upon a vision of an "alternative lifestyle"
containing far fewer amenities than Western industrial
societies presently provide. He notes that certain
products "are almost bound to be used in ways which are
damaging to community" (1982, p. 170) and uses as an
example the motorcar. Taylor does not emphasize,
however, the implicit costs of the trade-off he
proposes.

Hayek, in contrast to Taylor, is brutally frank
about what he sees to be the costs and benefits of a
retreat to community. The costs include most
fundamentally, a reduction in individual liberty, and
also a reduction in living standards, or a reduction in
population, or possibly both. The benefits might
include the satisfaction of certain emotional needs or
primitive instincts expressed by most individuals at
one time or another. Perhaps individuals may choose
community over the market society; such a choice and
its consequences are outlined more clearly by Hayek
than by Taylor.

Are there alternative visions of community to
interpose between anomic man in civil society and
solidarity in a transformed community? Hayek sketches
faint outlines of such an alternative. He does so by
reevaluating the possibilities for community to exist

within civil or market society.

Civil society is often regarded as containing individuals related not by shared symbols but rather coexisting on the basis of shared interdependencies (Vernon 1976). In Hayek's account, however, individuals do share not only common beliefs and values but also symbols. These shared symbols are anchored in and structured by the law.

Regarding the law, or rules of just conduct, as a set of symbols linking individuals together is a necessary step toward Hayek's understanding of law, tradition, and community. The community with which Hayek is concerned is a community held together by traditions of conduct which are passed from one generation to another. The body of law, changing with the problems of new generations, yet retaining the wisdom of the past generations, preserves a sense of community, even in a market society. The rise of commerce and the development of the abstract market society are commonly thought to destroy traditional ways of life. If we proceed from a Hayekian view of the law, the possibility emerges that the continuity of law counteracts the revolutionary nature of the changes capitalism brings. Once the closed community has been broken open, an evolving set of rules of conduct supplies the basis for the growth and development of the Great Society. What makes a community in advanced societies is "the common recognition of the same rules" (1979a, p. 40); but these rules themselves represent ties to the past and connections to the future.

As long as the law can be interpreted "as flowing out of the circumstances of society" (Parry 1982, p. 403), a consensus of habits, traditions, and customs, a shared sense of history, define the community. This is, of course, a vision originally and eloquently advanced by Burke.

> Because a nation is not an idea only of local extent, and individual momentary aggregation, but it is an idea of continuity, which extends in time as well as in numbers and space. And this is a choice not of one day, or one set of people, not a tumultuary or giddy choice; it is a deliberate election of ages and generations; it is a Constitution made by what is ten thousand times better than choice, it is made by the peculiar circumstances, occasions, tempers, dispositions, and moral, civil, and social habitudes of the people, which disclose themselves only in a long space of time (1884, vol. X, pp. 96-97).

Given this vision of the role of law for the preservation of a community, the greatest danger to that community arises when the law is viewed as purely arbitrary, or reflective of particular interests. The sense of community cannot be retained when the law fails to supply a broadly accepted set of shared symbols. This understanding of law explains Hayek's preoccupation with the law-making assembly in a democratic society. If the law is so crucial a factor in retaining consensus, then a democratic society is indeed playing with the factors of its own destruction when laws are commonly perceived to be the result of bargaining between interests.

COMPARISON WITH NOZICK

        In what respects would it be possible to reconcile the account of community provided by Hayek with that of the state of "utopia" provided in the work of Robert Nozick? I will argue here that a comparison of their views is helpful to illuminate the shared ground on which both authors stand. The differences between their understandings of the "metaframework" reveal not only philosophical differences between the two thinkers, but point out enduring dilemmas which community poses for liberal ideals. Neither Nozick nor Hayek claims to offer, or offers, solutions for these difficulties. Hayek's failure to do so allows us to pinpoint the shortcomings of his definition of individual liberty.
        The focus of my comparison will be on Nozick's chapter titled, "A Framework for Utopia" in Anarchy, State, and Utopia (1974). I will examine first two broad areas of agreement, then two topics on which the authors disagree. This chapter by Nozick reveals the similarities between epistemological foundations in the work of Nozick and Hayek. Nozick begins from the assumption that we can never formulate answers to all of our questions, nor design society in any one best way. "[G]iven our inability to formulate explicitly principles which adequately handle, in advance, all of the complex, multifarious stiuations which arise" (1974, p. 317), he contends that our attention should turn to "filtering processes." These processes (and Nozick refers directly to Hayek for illustration of how they are thought to work), when incorporated into a "metautopian" framework, leave room for "liberty for experimentation of varied sorts" (1974, p. 329). Hayek's own discussions arrive at similar conclusions, especially in terms of policy choices, as in The Constitution of Liberty, where many of his policy recommendations boil down to allowing experimentation to take place, in order to facilitate the best possible solution to a problem (see, for example, 1960, p. 355).

     In two related areas, however, Nozick and Hayek
part company. The aspects on which they differ are
subtle, and extremely important for the argument I make
in this book. Nozick is far more willing to consider
the notions of judgement and design than is Hayek.
While recognizing the limits of design by human beings,
Nozick also is quick to point out that filtering
processes are employed by human beings desirous of
design to the extent that it is possible--and
explicitly notes that filter devices need not be
thought incompatible with design devices. "Filtering
processes are especially appropriate for designers
having limited knowledge who do not know precisely the
nature of a desired end product....Nor need filter
devices exclude design aspects, especially in the
generating process" (1974, pp. 314, 315). People are
designers, according to Nozick's understanding--and as
such, they are also required to make judgements. "We
will have to leave room for people's judging each
particular instance" (1974, p. 318).
     Nozick and Hayek differ, then on the degree to
which they are comfortable with the notion of man the
designer, and ultimately with the focus of choice and
judgement. Thus, whereas Gray says of Hayek, "that the
processes of social life itself contain filter
devices...for the elimination of inadequate beliefs and
values" (1986, p. 115), Nozick looks at the long-run
view in the following way. "It is what grows
spontaneously from the individual choices of many
people over a long period of time that will be worth
speaking eloquently about" (1974, p. 332). The
difference, and Nozick's emphasis on the role of
individual choice, is evident when Nozick discusses the
"direction" of cultural evolution. The somewhat
dramatic and indeed ominous tone with which Hayek talks
about the dangers of messing about with cultural
traditions is absent in Nozick's discussion. He
distinguishes between biological and cultural evolution
by noting that due to historical memories and records,
"an already rejected alternative (or its slight
modification) can be retried, perhaps because new or
changed conditions make it now seem more promising or
appropriate" (1974, p. 317). The notion of judgement,
of capability on the part of individuals to assess when
previous strands of tradition have now become more
"appropriate," is implicit, and in a way that we do not
find without considerable equivocation in Hayek's work.
     The role of individual choice raises a host of
problems when we turn to look at the particular
communities of experimentation which could arise under
general frameworks. Hayek, like Nozick, is aware that
opting for decentralization for experimentation
purposes carries with it some weighty moral dilemmas.

Nozick alludes to "the perplexing questions" arising around decisions of a community to impose certain standards on its inhabitants, and acknowledges that the option of "exit," leaving the community to join or found another, is a costly and difficult choice. Hayek acknowledges in a similar fashion that questions of freedom in the small community are doubtless going to arise.

The questions Hayek raises have to do with the critical matter of how a community settles issues of membership. H. N. Hirsch notes that membership cannot be understood apart from "the exclusion of nonmembers [who] may be branded as heretics, or as genetically inferior, or as nonhuman barbarians, or as any of the countless other categories that have been invented for the 'nonmembers' of a community" (1986, p. 435). Hayek acknowledges these kinds of questions and admits he has no certain answers.

> One of the most difficult problems here is perhaps how the desire to attract or retain residents should and can be combined with a freedom of choice whom to accept and whom to reject as members of a particular community. Freedom of migration is one of the widely accepted and wholly admirable principles of liberalism. But should this generally give the stranger a right to settle down in a community in which he is not welcome?...Is this anti-liberal or morally justified? (1976, p. 195, n. 14)

The conflict between liberal goals and goals of community upon which Hayek touches here is posed in starker form when the work of contemporary communitarian critics of liberalism is examined. Can Hayek's concept of community built around a shared tradition of law suggest a satisfactory resolution to this conflict?

COMPARISON TO COMMUNITARIAN INSIGHTS

Communitarian critiques of liberalism are closely related to the "recovery" of insights associated with the tradition of civic humanism (Herzog 1986, p. 473). Amy Gutmann summarizes the communitarian criticisms in the following way.

> Like the critics of the 1960's, those of the 1980's fault liberalism for being mistakenly and irreparably individualistic. But the new wave of criticism is not a mere repetition of the old. Whereas the earlier critics were inspired by Marx,

the recent critics are inspired by Aristotle and Hegel (1985, p. 308).

There are two clearly discernible focuses of the communitarian critics, whose ranks include Michael Sandel, Alasdair MacIntyre, and Charles Taylor. One is the belief that "liberal individualism in its many guises as a social, economic, political and epistemological theory has critically misunderstood the relationship between individuals and their social being" (Doody 1984, p. 216). A second focus is an effort to recover the notion of community for contemporary liberal societies.

Characterizing communitarian critics' work in this way allows us to see the extent of and limits to the parallels between Hayek's work and the communitarians. Hayek asserts throughout his work that individuals must be regarded as social creatures whose existence is made possible by and is dependent upon the social context in which they find themselves. Hayek asserts that this conception of sociality behind individuality, and facilitating individuality, is genuinely liberal. Sheldon Wolin (1960) and Don Herzog (1986) agree that it is not the case that "instrumental rationality, presocial individuals, and so on...are integral to liberalism" (Herzog 1986, p. 480).[2] Hayek can be quite comfortable sharing the communitarian insistence that we cannot view individuals solely as unencumbered selves. However, it is not clear that Hayek and the communitarians agree on the nature of human sociality. For Hayek, the mediating stream which connects individuals is the stream of tacit knowledge, which has the capacity to flow down over the course of history as well as meander between individuals within a given culture. The stream of tacit knowledge, however, is not conceived by Hayek to supply either moral identity or moral education. More generally speaking, tacit knowledge is not the equivalent of the "politics of community" for prominent communitarians.

It is on the issue of the meaning of community that Hayek and the communitarians part company. For Hayek, the realms of politics and community touch, but ideally do so only in so far as political choices gently nudge shared rules of conduct in appropriate directions. As long as it remains limited, Hayek has no quarrel with the politics of interest. In short, he considers it essential for ordered liberty that the liberal self "is not, in some very basic way, touched or changed by political experience" (Hirsch 1986, p. 428).

Further differences emerge between Hayek and the communitarians when the communitarians turn to discussions of "virtue," or the "common good." For here, Hayek remains a firm believer in, as Gutmann puts it, the basic and necessary acceptance of nonshared ends characterizing a pluralist, free society. Hayek does not seem able to conceive of two different types of society which John Doody discusses, the society of unity but a "differentiated unity" versus a society along the lines of the tribal society from which Hayek believes we have evolved, a society of "undifferentiated unity." His inability to think about a society of "differentiated unity" is implicit in his failure to accord a role for individual judgement, or the use of critical reason in the evaluation of tradition and tacit knowledge. The consequences of avoiding judgement emerge when we compare Hayek and MacIntyre.

MACINTYRE AND THE LIMITS OF HAYEK'S SELF

There are two areas of agreement in MacIntyre and Hayek's writings which initially cloud the fundamental differences between them. MacIntyre argues nearly as forcefully as Hayek that we simply cannot know enough to attempt to "mold" social structures. "[T]he notion of social control embodied in the notion of expertise is indeed a masquerade. Our social order is in a very literal sense out of our, and indeed anyone's, control. No one is or could be in charge" (1984, p. 107). Social science has not been able to and cannot discover "laws" allowing sufficient predictability for manipulation of and control over society to occur.

MacIntyre's treatment of tacit knowledge and tradition is similar to that of Hayek. MacIntyre identifies one limited source of predictability in human affairs as tacit knowledge. "We all have a great deal of tacit, unspelled-out knowledge of the predictable expectations of others as well as a large stock of explicitly-stored information" (1984, p. 102). MacIntyre sees individuals both existing within and reasoning through traditions. Each person can be regarded as "one of the bearers of a tradition....all reasoning takes place within the context of some traditional mode of thought, transcending through criticism and invention the limitations of what had hitherto been reasoned in that tradition" (pp. 221-222).

Despite these surface similarities, MacIntyre and Hayek understand tradition differently. A bearer of tradition, for MacIntyre, is a bearer of a <u>social identity</u>. Our lives and our particular histories derive meaning or intelligibility <u>through</u> the histories of traditions. Tacit knowledge and tradition make sense of life for the self in MacIntyre; for Hayek the

self seems to stand separate from tacit knowledge,
routinely dipping into or using tacit knowledge, to be
sure, but disengaged from it. And tacit knowledge is
not seen to convey "meaning" in Hayek's work. The term
meaning itself appears anomalous in his thought, given
his limited conception of human purposiveness.   In
addition, from The Sensory Order onward, Hayek denies
there is any such thing as a whole greater than the sum
of the parts. MacIntyre, however, speaks confidently
of how "a life may be more than a sequence of
individual actions and episodes" (1984, p. 204).

Finally, MacIntyre offers an account of how
traditions may be sustained and preserved that goes
beyond anything in Hayek's writing. In order for
traditions to continue to convey meaning requires
judgement as well as virtue. Judgement here refers to
"knowing how to select among the relevant stack of
maxims and how to apply them in particular situations"
(1984, p. 223). Such a clear account never emerges in
Hayek, although intimations of it can be found.
MacIntyre's concept of virtue, however, is completely
alien to Hayek. For virtue in MacIntyre's account has
a social as well as personal character, for it sustains
what MacIntyre calls practices.

MacIntyre defines a practice in the following way.

A practice is any coherent and complex form of
socially established cooperative human activity
through which goods internal to that form of
activity are realized in the course of trying to
achieve those standards of excellence which are
appropriate to, and partially definitive of, that
form of activity, with the result that human
powers to achieve excellence, and human
conceptions of the ends and goods involved, are
systematically extended (1984, p. 187).

Internal goods are not just an individual's possession,
but represent a good for all those, that is, the
community, which participate in a practice. Because
practices have histories, participants "cannot be
initiated into a practice without accepting the
authority of the best standards realized so far" (1984,
p. 190). Submission is necessary in order to acquire
judgement and in order to advance the practice itself.
Furthermore, to engage in the relationships with others
necessary if one is to participate in a practice
requires the exercise of virtues--justice, honesty,
courage.

One can argue that the use of reason to sustain
and enlarge freedom in Hayek's work appears to be one
kind of a practice. To succeed in the use of reason,
he contends, requires accepting a history and body of

thought which has gone before, as well as the inherent
limitations of human reason. He even gives an account
of "individualist" virtues resembling those of
MacIntyre. But Hayek, like the eighteenth-century
writers MacIntyre discusses, lacks any view of
community allowing for a shared concept of tradition
and supportive virtues.

> [They] treat of society as nothing more than an
> arena in which individuals seek to secure what is
> useful or agreeable to them... [excluding from
> view]....any conception of society as a community
> united in a shared vision of the good for
> man...and a <u>consequent</u> shared practice of the
> virtues" (MacIntyre 1984, p. 236)

There is no basis in Hayek for the regard for "internal
goods" that both demands and makes meaningful the
virtues. Individual liberty remains therefore
exclusively defined in terms of "external goods," and
individual freedom remains of necessity freedom against
community rather than freedom in community.

In order to advance toward a final assessment of
Hayek's understanding of liberty, and directions for
revision of that understanding, I wish to summarize and
comment upon the differences between Hayek and
MacIntyre. Hayek fits clearly within the liberal
individualist tradition MacIntyre critiques. The
essence of the alternative MacIntyre seeks to recover
has to do with a competing vision of community. The
idea of community in the modern liberal view is that a
liberal state provides "the arena in which each
individual seeks his or her own private good" (1984, p.
172). In contrast, MacIntyre argues a case for the
necessity for a good human life of viewing community as
the place "in which men in company pursue the human
good (1984, p. 172). Hayek rejects any such effort to
define "the human good," basing his rejection on the
belief that such a definition carries with it,
inevitably, a case for enforcement of undifferentiated
unity.

My own position is that it is possible to conceive
of public agreement on the nature of the good life
which neither commits us to a shared vision of ends,
either natural or otherwise justified, nor to a society
of undifferentiated unity. And our understanding of
how such an agreement can be reached can benefit from
the ways in which the concept of the self in Hayek's
liberal theory approaches the understanding of the
situated self in MacIntyre. Three parts of MacIntyre's
concept of the situated self are strikingly similar to
Hayek's definition of the self as a cultural being:
(1) the self can never choose what standpoint to

adopt--that is given, and cannot arbitrarily be selected; (2) the self always enters upon a stage and plays parts in ongoing dramas as a co-author; and (3) the self is a bearer of tradition. For both thinkers, a measure of uncritical submission to cultural practices is necessary. What remains equally unclear in both conceptions is the point at which critical reflection and sifting begins. Without treatment of this topic, it is unclear if and when individuals emerge as autonomous beings engaged in the making of moral judgements.

SUMMARY AND PROPOSAL

In this last section of the book, I attempt to accomplish two goals. The first is to assess the whole of Hayek's philosophy, and indicate where I find that philosophy lacking. The second is to sketch an alternative perspective on individual liberty which draws upon both the strengths and weaknesses (as suggestive of areas requiring attention) of Hayek's work. My claim is simply that my alternative may help to advance our thinking about how communitarian kinds of insights can supplement traditional and highly valued liberal ways of thinking about individual autonomy.

Hayek's philosophy is incoherent because of three flawed areas in his work on which his concept of ordered liberty is based. The first area is his consideration of tacit knowledge. In his preoccupation with questions of survival and practical skills, Hayek fails to see that tacit knowledge contains another and equally important dimension. This is the dimension of "internal prosperity," or answers to the question of "how to survive and live a good life." Tacit knowledge contains a wealth of information and "commonsense" understandings about how, as human beings, we make some sense of our existence. This includes how individuals come to peace with some of the aspects of the life they lead, even while accepting that we may never fully come to terms with the ambiguities of the difficult choices we face as individuals and members of communities as well.

I believe that Hayek follows firmly in the modern tradition in this narrow conception of the content of tacit knowledge. Despite his criticism of Descartes and other constructivist rationalist thinkers, Hayek falls into a mode of thought tracing its roots to Descartes. The prevalence of this mode of thought amongst academics in general and social scientists in particular tends to blind us to its implications for philosophy and discussions of the meaning of life.

Hayek's skeptical epistemology positions him firmly in the rationalist tradition of philosophy. The highly plausible insistence of the "strictly limited" reach of the human mind was followed by a common but unnecessary curtailment of interest in matters of "wholes" beyond that limited reach. E. F. Schumacher describes this tendency of modern philosophy in the following way.

> While traditional wisdom had considered the human mind as weak but open-ended--that is, capable of reaching beyond itself toward higher and higher levels--the new thinking took it as axiomatic that the mind's reach had fixed and narrow limits, which could be clearly determined, while within these limits it possessed virtually unlimited powers (1977, p. 10).

Hayek disagrees, of course, that within its limits the mind possesses unlimited powers; but his philosophy reveals the same neglect of the possibilities of "reaching beyond" as the rest of post-Descartes European philosophy.

The narrow conception of tacit knowledge characterizing Hayek's work plays itself out in another significant way. This is in his shallow discussion of the problems posed by the dominant moral code of the market society. He tells us that morals, in the last analysis, rest upon the esteem which individuals grant to one another. In Hayek's interpretation, in the early history of developing market societies esteem was granted to those who demonstrated they could plan ahead, take care of their families, and acquire wealth to make possible continued care. Whether this was in fact the case I will not attempt to suggest here; however, in the advanced catallactic economies of the West, Hayek acknowledges that one cannot base judgements of moral esteem upon simple financial gain. The factors of luck, structural change, and changing tastes in society make it clear that market success need not reflect any particularly "virtuous," and therefore esteemable behavior. Money cannot be regarded as the basis for esteem without considerable effort to ignore the workings of modern societies.

Esteem and morality are further complicated in market societies by the fact that when one enters a market transaction, one must implicitly trust that the partners in the exchange will be honest or at least can be held accountable. This implies that in market societies, one must act as if one believes all other actors are honorable, even while recognizing and endeavoring to decipher the presence of dishonorable characters. Yet few could disagree with Hayek's declaration that "the demand that we should equally esteem all our fellow men is irreconcilable with the fact that our whole moral code rests on the approval or disapproval of the conduct of others" (1976, p. 99). The making of moral judgements in market societies is confusing and difficult.

My point is not to claim that these problems dictate that we must somehow "turn the clock back." It is rather to point out that we must by necessity turn to interactions and relationships that are not strictly exchange or market dominated, if we are to continue to exercise moral judgement. (An alternative point of view is to say that a great many people in fact simply suspend the effort to make such moral judgements; I am not persuaded that this is true, although I do believe that morality is often problematical, and experienced as such, in market societies.) Nonmarket mechanisms and institutions, including word-of-mouth, friendships, "gossip," and institutions designed to gather information and complaints of interest to consumers generally, supplement our involvement in market relationships. Tacit knowledge, I contend, contains veins of knowledge that serve to keep some moral perspective intact--and this function of tacit knowledge is fully as important as, if not more important than, the practical, "how-to" knowledge Hayek describes.

The importance of the gradual shifting of stores of tacit knowledge is precisely that in its dynamic aspects, tacit knowledge aids adjustment through successive stages of market development. This brings us to the second area of weakness in Hayek's presentation, that related to his discussion of cultural evolution. Especially in his most recent work, Hayek focuses almost exclusively on the "wisdom" of cultural evolution and the ability of culture to "direct" our lives, if we will only let it. Indeed, Hayek's main plea in these recent writings is that we must bow before the wisdom and authority of cultural traditions.

This perspective arises because of Hayek's failure to consider two eminently plausible perspectives on cultural traditions that ought to temper his views. One is the perspective noted in the work of MacIntyre, which is that any healthy tradition embodies conflicts about the precise meanings it conveys. From this perspective, it is simply not possible to sit back and "obey" tradition. The ambiguities and indeed contrasting elements of traditional knowledge do not present clear-cut choices that individuals can unreflectively adopt.

The focus on culture as a guiding principle for the channeling of human action which typifies Hayek's latest work reflects the absence of a second perspective on the processes of cultural development and change. As Richard Barrett (1984) succinctly describes culture, there are two opposed tendencies or processes going on in every society and in every historical period. One is what Barrett refers to as "regularization processes," the "effort to impose rules and order, and to make the rules binding on others. Rules in this sense have an inhibiting, channeling, or deterrent effect on behavior" (1984, p. 213). The second is "situational adjustment," in which rules tend to _follow_ behavior. "No matter how sensibly the rules are drawn, they must be applied to complex and untidy circumstances. Moreover the circumstances do not remain constant" (1984, p. 211), and as circumstances change, so do people's actions--in some cases, whether the rules have changed or not. Just as tacit knowledge reflects expertise related to particulars of time and place, so too do cultural traditions both shape and follow individual behaviors. If cultural traditions do not change, they are likely to stagnate. To advocate following cultural traditions as if they are some ascertainable and unchanging source of wisdom is to oversimplify their nature and ignore the role of the individual in cultural change.

The third major difficulty in Hayek's philosophy, his inability to confront the uncertainties of the nature of human agency, is reflected in his inability to see individual human actions changing cultural traditions. The relationships of man to nature and to other individuals cannot be authoritatively "grounded" in any indisputable principles. Ronald Beiner suggests that every modern philosopher after Kant has to confront the "requirement that one bear up to an absolutely _alien_ nature at the same time as one exalts one's own absolute freedom in this alienated condition" (1984, p. 359). Nature is no longer the source of knowledge of the "good life" for humans, as it was in Aristotle. Conceptions of the good life must be supplied by individual human beings if they are to remain autonomous yet establish a place for themselves in the overarching order of life. Beiner argues that most modern philosophers have "sought in the end 'a return to security,' rather than facing up to the task of finding a home among men in this situation of ontological homelessness" (1984, p. 359).

Does Hayek fit in the category of philosophers who ultimately seek a return to security? I believe that he does, and that his increasing pessimism about human rationality and the gloomy calls for turning to the past of cultural tradition reflect his unwillingness to confront the fact that human choice is, in the last analysis, unpredictable. The freedom of modern market societies Hayek holds so dear may not be sustained by individuals in the future; the discipline of the marketplace, the ambiguity and complexity of moral choice in that environment, and the painful autonomy it seems to require, may lead to a rejection of individual liberty. Yet instead of bravely acknowledging that the liberal society of individual freedom is a perilous course, and one requiring a great deal of commitment and judgement, as he did in his early work, the older Hayek appears content to warn against the folly we are all too likely to commit. By failing to come to terms with the essential and dominant role to be played by human choice, by human agency, in the shaping of traditions and morality, he undercuts the values he most wishes to defend. For with recognition of the ultimately individualist nature of judgement, one not only accepts the fundamental unpredictability of the course of human history, one also affirms the dignity and potential of individual human beings to, together, shape the world in which they live.

I propose we recognize that individual judgements reflect a complex process involving not only the exercise of critical rationality, but also the responsible assessment of the evolutionary factors which make human choice and human freedom possible. It may be helpful to think of judgement emanating from, or reflecting the culmination of a three-level framework of choice. At the most fundamental level, our thinking and being are intertwined with fundamental pretheoretical convictions or intuitions which we can never fully know or understand. At the next level, one closer to the surface, is a set of "decontextualized statements," or generalized rules of behavior. Culturally distinguishable, in my opinion, these statements include rules of obligation or prohibition. "[P]assed down from century to century, from society to society, the generalized, decontextualized statement becomes the touchstone of moral rationality" (Goody 1980, p. 161). At this level we find statements including wisdom about how individuals have lived together in peaceful or productive or happy fashion in the social groups without which advanced civilization is impossible.

The third level, upon which most of us probably operate on a day-to-day basis, involves learned or devised "rules of context" for decontextualized statements. Taken together, such rules of context are systems of application concerning when, where, and how to apply general rules. An example originally used by John Goody in a different context seems to illustrate this layer well. Given "thou shalt not kill" as a general rule, certain traditions of behavior interpret the rule. The rule is followed in certain specified contexts and is not followed in others, allowing the

rule to become "thou shalt not kill unless they have
done you harm, or except in times of war, or unless
they are criminals" (Goody 1980, p. 161). It can
readily be seen that these cultural specifications can
change content over time and according to different
environments, allowing for varying applications of the
rule.
     Recognizing that this third layer of the structure
does not stay the same, but can change rapidly as well
as gradually, brings us to the role played by
"rational" or purposive ethical choice. Individuals
engage in a process of evaluating whether or not
learned rules of context satisfactorily interpret
decontextualized statements. "[C]ontinuously new
derivation and refoundation of norms by rational
reasoning by every individual has to probe in each
generation the continuing validity of traditional
knowledge crystallized in norms" (Markl, 1980, p. 226).
The continuing unknown factor--and the agent of
change--is the reasoning of many independent, free
individuals.
     For such individuals to be truly autonomous, then,
in the sense of which I have spoken, is to say that
individuals are free when they are able to engage in
the process of considering the traditional sources of
their morals, values, and practices, while reflecting
upon what morals they choose to hold as individuals.
This implies recognition that one is indeed situated in
and dependent upon choices previously made in the
communities and traditions of which one is a part.
They supply a tacit context which must be acknowledged
and embraced if people are to act wisely as individuals
as well as members of communities in the choice
situations they encounter. If the tacit context is
accepted but never critiqued and thus transcended in
some fashion, then true autonomy, and with it, the
liberal society, cannot exist. Given awareness of the
tacit context, the primacy of the individual remains,
but it is a primacy softened by and supplemented by the
realization that meaning is constituted in some
relationship to and with the norms of one's community
and traditions. Autonomy in my sense then approaches
John Gray's definition of the autonomous man: "the
critical and self-critical man whose allegiance to his
society's norms is informed by the best exercise of his
rational powers" (1986a, p. 60).
     This supplementary view of the human condition
simultaneously softens and strengthens liberal visions
of individual freedom. The traditional backdrop of
Western culture, or indeed of any culture, is given
notice as constituting an essential basis of individual
liberty. While this view forces us to see that "all
choices are conditioned by the community we belong to,

by our membership, role and function within that
community," and that we are thus "in fact only the
co-creator, the co-authors of our own lives," (Doody
1984, p. 219), it does not justify retreat from
critical consideration of the forces with which we
co-author our life stories. My own view is that it in
fact points with more urgency to examination of those
forces, the structures of the community, the meaning of
the traditions, within which we co-create our lives.

This view also confronts us with the fundamental
moral ambiguity of human beings, which is to recognize
the limits of the extent to which we can chart our own
lives, while bearing full responsibility for the
efforts we ourselves make to shape our destinies. The
tension of balancing individual perceptions and
conceptions with the many and often confusing
interpretations we imbibe from social structure and
cultural traditions presents the inevitable environment
in which free choice is meaningful. The unique feature
of the liberal society then becomes awareness of the
presence and complexity of balancing the needs for
community and individualism. Substituting the terms
"public" and "private" for community and individualism,
William Galston formulates a similar assessment of
liberal society.

> The autonomy of the private is incomplete; the
> public and the private are linked in a complex web
> of reciprocal impact and dependence. Accordingly,
> the achievement of appropriate relations between
> them is an endless task of imperfect adjustment.
> But at least liberal societies, unlike most
> others, are conscious of the necessity of this
> task and build this consciousness into their
> guiding principles and basic institutions (1982,
> p. 629).

Such a perspective on liberal society indicates
that our tasks are both to "look inward" and assess
what our tacit body of knowledge tells us about
practical existence and the meaningful conduct of life,
and to "look outward" in an ongoing empirical quest to
discover the consequences for individual liberty and
community of traditional moralities as well as
constitutional and political rules of the game. The
costs and the investments are high, and it is clear
that the rewards of such investigations are always
unpredictable. We cannot hope to be the "sole author"
of our lives, but once that hope is set aside, freedom
can hold the promise of significant autonomy and
self-conscious direction. This kind of freedom rests
upon appreciation for and willingness to work within
the context of our many relationships with other people

that, taken in its entirety, constitutes the elusive part of our lives we know as community. The risks of immersion in community, and the intolerance and oppression which result, can similarly never be precluded as one possibility for our future. But a vision of freedom involving critical, ongoing examination of the many facets of that community offers us a liberal account of the good life that blends the insights of a communitarian perspective with the liberal insistence on the dignity of individual choice. Both individual freedom and the flourishing of the individual within the context of community become the intertwined ideals of liberalism.

NOTES

1.   For a forthright discussion on the perils of turning the state into a national community in order to meet emotional needs, see Hirsch (1986).
2.   Notably, Herzog cites David Hume as one who "scoffs at the myth of presocial individuals" (1986, p. 480).

Bibliography

Acton, H.B. 1961. Objectives. In Agenda for a free society. Ed. A. Seldon. London: Hutchison and Company.
———. 1952. Prejudice. Revue Internationale de Philosophie 21:323-336.
Adair, D. 1957. 'That politics may be reduced to a science,' David Hume, James Madison, and the Tenth Federalist. Huntington Library Quarterly 20:343-360.
Alchian, A. 1950. Uncertainty, evolution, and economic theory. Journal of Political Economy 58:211-221.
Allen, D.Y. 1981. Modern conservatism: the problem of definition. Review of Politics 43:582-603.
Arnold, R. 1980. Hayek and institutional evolution. Journal of Libertarian Studies 4:341-351.
Bailyn, B. 1967. The ideological origins of the American revolution. Cambridge: University of Massachusetts Press.
Banfield, E. 1964. In defense of the American party system. In Political Parties, USA. Ed. R.A. Goldwin. Chicago: Rand McNally.
Barrett, R. 1984. Culture and conduct: an excursion in anthropology. Belmont, California: Wadsworth.
Barrington, D. 1954. Edmund Burke as an economist. Economica 21:252-258.
Barry, N. 1979. Hayek's social and economic philosophy. London: Macmillan.
———. 1981. An introduction to modern political theory. New York: St. Martin's Press.
———. 1983. Review article: the new liberalism. British Journal of Political Science 13:93-123.
———. 1984. Hayek on liberty. In conceptions of liberty in political philosophy. Ed. Z. Pelczynski and J. Gray. London: Athlone Press.
Barth, H. 1960. The idea of order: contributions to

the philosophy of politics. Dordrecht: D. Reidel
Publishing Company.
Baumgarth, W.P.   1978.   Hayek and political order: the
rule of law.   Journal of Libertarian Studies
2:11-28.
Bay, C.   1971.   Hayek's liberalism: the constitution
of perpetual privilege.   Political Science
Reviewer 1:93-124.
Beiner, R.   1984.   Action, natality, and citizenship:
Hannah Arendt's concept of freedom.   In
Conceptions of liberty in political philosophy.
Ed. Z. Pelczynski and J. Gray.   London: Athlone
Press.
Berlin, I.   1969.   Four essays on liberty.   Oxford:
Oxford University   Press.
Bevan, R.A.   1973.   Marx and Burke: a revisionist
view.   LaSalle, Ill.: Open Court Publishing Co.
Bosanquet, N.   1983.   Economics: after the new right.
Boston: Kluwer-Nijhoff Publishing.
Bourke, P.F.   1975.   The pluralist reading of James
Madison's Tenth Federalist.   Perspectives in
American History 11:271-295.
Branson, R.   1979.   James Madison and the Scottish
Enlightenment.   Journal of the History of Ideas
40:233-250.
Bredvold, L.I.   1961.   The brave new world of the
enlightenment.   Ann Arbor: University of Michigan
Press.
Bredvold, L. and Ross, R.   1960.   The philosophy of
Edmund Burke.   Ann Arbor: University of Michigan
Press.
Bridwell, R. and Whitten, R.   1977.   The Constitution
and the common law: the decline of the doctrines
of separation of powers and federalism.
Lexington, Mass.: D.C. Heath and Company.
Brittan, S.   1980.   Hayek, the new right, and the
crisis of social democracy.   Encounter 54:30-46.
————.   1983.   The role and limits of government.
Essays in political economy.   Minneapolis:
University of Minnesota Press.
————.   1984.   The wisdom of the market. [Review
Article] Times   L i t e r a r y
Supplement.   No. 4223, March 9: 235-236.
Buchanan, J.M.   1975.   The limits of liberty.   Chicago:
University of Chicago Press.
————.   1977.   Law and the invisible hand.   In Freedom
in constitutional contract: perspectives of a
political economist.   College Station: Texas A&M
University Press.
————.   1982.   Cultural evolution and institutional
reform.   Paper presented to Liberty Fund
Conference, March.
Buchanan, J.M. and Tullock, G.   1962.   The calculus of

consent.   Ann   Arbor: University   of   Michigan
Press.
Burke, E.   1884.   The works of Edmund Burke.   12
volumes. Boston: Little, Brown, and Company.
————.   1973.   Reflections on the revolution in
France. Garden City, N.Y.   Doubleday Press.
Burns, E.M.   1968.   James Madison philosopher of the
constitution. New York: Octagon Books.
Butler, E.   1983.   Hayek: his contribution to the
political and economic thought of our time.   New
York: Universe Books.
Campbell, D.   1975.   On   the   conflicts   between
biological   and   social   evolution   and   between
psychology   and   moral   tradition.   American
Psychologist 30:1103-1126.
————.   1979.   Comments on the sociobiology of ethics
and moralizing. Behavioral Science 24: 37-45.
————.   1980. Social morality norms as evidence of
conflict   between   biological   human   nature   and
social   system   requirements.   In   Morality as a
biological phenomenon.   Ed. G.S. Stent.   Berkeley:
University of California Press, pp. 67-82.
Campbell, J.A.   1970.   Edmund Burke: argument from
circumstance in Reflections on the Revolution in
France.   Studies   in   Burke   and   His   Time
12:1764-1784.
Canavan, F.P.   1960.   The political reason of Edmund
Burke. Durham: Duke   University Press.
Carey, G.W.   1976.   Majority tyranny and the extended
republic   theory   of   James   Madison.   Modern Age
20:40-53.
Chapman, G.W.   1967.   Edmund   Burke: the   practical
imagination.   Cambridge: Harvard   University
Press.
Cone, C.B. 1964. Burke and the European social order.
Thought 39:273-288.
Conniff, J.   1975.   On the obsolescence of the general
will: Rousseau,   Madison   and   the   evolution   of
republican political thought.   Western Political
Quarterly 28:32-58.
————.   1977.   Burke,   Bristol   and   the   concept   of
representation.   Western   Political   Quarterly
30:329-341.
Cragg, A.W. 1983.   Hayek, justice and the market.
Canadian Journal of Philosophy 13:563-568.
Cristi, F.   1984.   Hayek and Schmitt on the rule of
law.   Canadian   Journal   of   Political   Science
17:521-535.
Cunningham, R.L., ed. 1979.   Liberty and the rule of
law. College Station: Texas A&M University Press.
deCrespigny, A.   1976.   Freedom   for   progress.   In
Contemporary   political   philosophers.   Eds.   A.
deCrespigny and K. Minogue. London: Methuen.

Diamond, A. 1980. F.A. Hayek on constructivism and
ethics. The Journal of Libertarian Studies 4:353-
366.
Diamond, M. 1959. Democracy and the Federalist: a
reconsideration of the framers' intent. American
Journal of Political Science 53:52-68.
————. 1975. The revolution of sober expectations.
In The American revolution: three views. New
York: American Brands, Inc.
Dinwiddy, J.R. 1974-1975. Utility and natural law in
Burke's thought: a reconsideration. Studies in
Burke and His Time 16:105-128.
————. 1978. Burke and the Utilitarians: a
rejoinder. Studies in Burke and His Time
19:119-126.
Doody, J.A. 1984. Recent reconstructings of political
philosophy. Philosophy Today 28:215-228.
Draper, T. 1982. Hume and Madison: the secrets of
Federalist Paper No. 10.   E n c o u n t e r
58:34-47.
Dreyer, F.A. 1979. Burke's politics: a study in Whig
orthodoxy. Waterloo, Ontario: Wilfrid Laurier
University Press.
Dunn, W.C. 1941. Adam Smith and Edmund Burke:
complimentary contemporaries. Southern Economic
Journal 7:330-346.
Dyer, P.W. and Hickman, R.H. 1979. American
conservatism and F.A. Hayek. Modern Age
23:381-393.
Eidelberg, P. 1968. The philosophy of the American
constitution. New York: Free Press.
Einaudi, M. 1934. The British background of Burke's
political thought. Political Science Quarterly
49:576-598.
Elster, J. 1983. Sour grapes: studies in the
subversion of rationality. Cambridge: Cambridge
University Press.
Fasel, G. 1976. 'The soul that animated': the role
of property in Burke's thought. Studies in Burke
and His Time 17:27-42.
Forbes, D. 1976. Sceptical Whiggism, commerce, and
liberty. In Essays on Adam Smith. Eds. A.
Skinner and T. Wilson. Oxford: Oxford University
Press.
Freeman, M. 1980. Edmund Burke and the critique of
political radicalism. Chicago: University of
Chicago Press.
Friedrich, C.J., ed. 1962. Liberty. Nomos, No. 4.
Yearbook of the American Society for Political and
Legal Philosophy. New York: Lieber-Alberton.
Galston, W. 1982. Defending liberalism. American
Political Science Review 76:621-629.
Goody, J. 1980. Literacy and moral rationality. In

Morality as a biological phenomenon. Ed. G.S.
Stent. Berkeley: University of California Press.
Gordon, S. 1981. The political economy of F.A. Hayek.
Canadian Journal of Economics 14:470-487.
Gould, S. 1980. The panda's thumb. New York: W.W.
Norton.
Grafstein, R. 1981. The problem of choosing your
alternatives: a revision of the public choice
theory of constitutions. Social Science Quarterly
62:199-212.
Gray, J. 1980. F.A. Hayek on liberty and tradition.
Journal of Libertarian Studies 4:121-137.
————. 1981. Hayek on liberty, rights and justice.
Ethics 92:73-84.
————. 1986. Hayek on liberty. Oxford: Basil
Blackwell.
————. 1986a. Liberalism. Milton Keynes, England:
Open University Press.
Gutmann, A. 1985. Communitarian critics of
liberalism. Philosophy and Public Affairs 14:308-
322.
Gwyn, W.B. 1965. The meaning of the separation of
powers. New Orleans: Tulane University.
Hamowy, R. 1971. Freedom and the rule of law in F.A.
Hayek. Il Politico 36:349-377.
————. 1978. Law and the liberal society: F.A.
Hayek's constitution of liberty. Journal of
Libertarian Studies 2:287-297.
Harrod, R. 1946. Professor Hayek on individualism.
Economic Journal 56:435-442.
Hart, J. 1967. Burke and radical freedom. Review of
Politics 29:221-238.
Hayek, F.A. 1944. The road to serfdom. Chicago:
University of Chicago Press.
————. 1948. Individualism and economic order.
Chicago: University of Chicago Press.
————. 1952. The sensory order: an inquiry into the
foundation of theoretical psychology. London:
Routledge and Kegan Paul.
————. 1952a. The counter-revolution of science.
Glencoe, Ill.: Free Press.
————, ed. 1954. Capitalism and the historians.
Chicago: University of Chicago Press.
————. 1955. The political ideal of the rule of law.
Cairo: National Bank of Egypt.
————. 1960. The constitution of liberty. Chicago:
University of Chicago Press.
————. 1967. Studies in philosophy, politics, and
economics. Chicago: University of Chicago Press.
————. 1973. Rules and order. Vol. I of Law,
legislation, and liberty: a new statement of the
liberal principles of justice and political
economy. Chicago: University of Chicago Press.

————. 1975. Economics, politics and freedom: an
interview with F.A. Hayek. Reason 6:4-12.
————. 1976. The mirage of social injustice. Vol.
II of Law, legislation, and liberty: a new
statement of the liberal principles of justice and
political economy. Chicago: University of
Chicago Press.
————. 1978. New studies in philosophy, politics,
economics, and the history of ideas. Chicago:
University of Chicago Press.
————. 1978a. The miscarriage of the democratic
ideal. Encounter 50:14-17.
————. 1978b. Denationalization of money. London:
Institute of Economic Affairs.
————. 1979. The political order of a free people.
Vol. III of Law, legislation, and liberty: a new
statement of the liberal principles of justice and
political economy. Chicago: University of
Chicago Press.
————. 1979a. The reactionary character of the
socialist conception. Lecture delivered at
Stanford University, 27 October 1978. Stanford:
Hoover Institution on War, Revolution, and Peace.
————. 1979b. Social justice, socialism and
democracy: three Australian lectures.
Turramurra, Australia: Center for Independent
Studies.
————. 1983. Knowledge, evolution, and society.
London: Adam Smith Institute.
————. 1983a. An interview with F.A. Hayek December
1, 1982. Policy Report 5:5-9.
————. 1984. The origins and effects of our morals:
a problem for science. In The essence of Hayek.
Ed. C. Nishiyama and K. Leube. Stanford,
California: Stanford University Press.
Hayek's 'Serfdom' revisited. 1984. London: Institute
of Economic Affairs.
Herberg, W. 1959. Natural law and history in Burke's
thought. Modern Age 3:325-328.
Herzog, D. 1986. Some questions for republicans.
Political Theory 14:473-493.
Hill, B.W., ed. 1975. Edmund Burke on government,
politics, and society. New York: International
Publications Service.
Hirsch, H.N. 1986. The threnody of liberalism:
constitutional liberty and the renewal of
community. Political Theory 14:423-449.
Hirschman, A.O. 1977. The passions and the interests.
Princeton: Princeton University Press.
Hobson, C.F. 1979. The negative on state laws: James
Madison, the constitution and the crisis of
republican government. William and Mary Quarterly
36:215-235.

Hoffman, R.J.S. and Levack, P., eds. 1949. Burke's
    politics. New York: Alfred A. Knopf.
Hoy, C. 1984. A philosophy of individual
    freedom. Westport, Conn.: Greenwood Press.
Hutchins, R.M. 1943. The theory of oligarchy: Edmund
    Burke. Thomist 5:61-78.
————. 1943. The theory of the state: Edmund Burke.
    Review of Politics 5:139-55.
Ingersoll, D.E. 1970. Machiavelli and Madison:
    perspectives on political stability. Political
    Science Quarterly 85:259-280.
Johnson, Warren. 1979. Muddling toward frugality.
    Boulder: Shambhala.
Kenyon, C.M. 1955. Men of little faith: the
    anti-Federalists on the nature of representative
    government. William and Mary Quarterly 12:3-43.
Ketcham, R. 1958. James Madison and the nature of
    man. Journal of the History of Ideas 19:62-76.
Kilcup, R.W. 1979. Reason and the basis of morality
    in Burke. Journal of the History of Philosophy
    17:271-284.
Kirk, R. 1953. The conservative mind from Burke to
    Santayana. Chicago: Henry Regnery Company.
————. 1967. Edmund Burke: a genius reconsidered.
    New Rochelle: Arlington House.
————. 1969. Enemies of the permanent things. New
    Rochelle: Arlington House.
————. 1974. The roots of american order. LaSalle,
    Ill.: Open Court Publishing Co.
Kiser, T. and E. Ostrom. 1982. The three worlds of
    action: a metatheoretical synthesis of
    institutional approaches. In Strategies of polit-
    ical inquiry. Ed. E. Ostrom. Beverly Hills:
    Sage Publications.
Kitwood, T. 1983. 'Personal identity' and personal
    integrity. In Morality in the making. Ed. H.
    Weinreich-Haste and D. Locke. New York: John
    Wiley and Sons.
Knight, F. 1949. Natural law: last refuge of the
    bigot. Ethics 59:127-135.
————. 1967. Laissez faire: pro and con. Journal
    of Political Economy 75:782-795.
Koch, A. 1950. Jefferson and Madison: the great
    collaboration. New York: Alfred A. Knopf.
Kramnick, I. 1970. Skepticism in English political
    thought: from Temple to Burke. Studies in Burke
    and His Time 12:1627-1661.
————. 1983. The Left and Edmund Burke. Political
    Theory 11:189-214.
Kristol, I. 1970. 'When virtue loses all her
    loveliness'-Some reflections on capitalism and
    'the free society'. The Public Interest 17:3-15.
Kundera, M. 1981. The book of laughter and

forgetting. New York: Penguin Books.
Lachmann, L.M. 1976. On the central concept of
Austrian economics: market process. In The
foundations of modern Austrian economics. Ed. E.
Dolan. Kansas City: Sheed and Ward.
Laski, H.J. 1948. Political thought in England: Locke
to Bentham. London: Oxford University Press.
Lerner, R. 1979. Commerce and character: the
Anglo-American as new-model man. William and Mary
Quarterly 36:3-26.
Letwin, S. 1976. The achievement of Friedrich A.
Hayek. In Essays on Hayek. Ed. F. Machlup. New
York: New York University Press, pp. 147-170.
Lindgren, J.R. 1973. The Social Philosophy of Adam
Smith. The Hague: Martinus Nijhoff.
Lumsden, C.J. and Wilson, E.O. 1983. Promethean fire:
reflections on the origin of mind. Cambridge:
Harvard University Press.
Macbeth, N. 1971. Darwin retried: an appeal to
reason. Boston: Gambit Incorporated.
MacCullum, G.C., Jr. 1967. Negative and positive
freedom. Philosophical Review 76:312-334.
Macfie, A.L. 1967. The individual in society.
London: George Allen and Unwin.
Machan, T.R. 1979. Reason, morality, and the free
society. In Liberty and the rule of law. Ed.
R.L. Cunningham. College Station: Texas A&M
University Press.
Machlup, F., ed. 1976. Essays on Hayek. New York:
New York University Press.
MacIntyre, A. 1984. After virtue: a study in moral
theory. Notre Dame, Indiana: University of Notre
Dame Press.
Mack, E. 1984. Hayek on justice and the market: a
reply to Macleod. Canadian Journal of Philosophy
13:569-574.
Macleod, A.M. 1984. Justice and the market. Canadian
Journal of Philosophy 13:551-562.
————. 1984. "Hayek on Justice and the Market: A
Rejoinder to Cragg and Mack." Canadian Journal of
Philosophy 13:575-584.
Macneil, I.R. 1986. Exchange revisited: individual
utility and social solidarity. Ethics 96:567-593.
Macpherson, C.B. 1978. Property. Toronto:
University of Toronto Press.
————. 1980. Burke. New York: Hill and Wang.
Maddox, G. 1982. A note on the meaning of
'constitution.' American Political Science Review
76:805-809.
Madison, J. 1901. The papers of James Madison.
Washington: Langtree and O'Sullivan.
————. 1961. The federalist papers. Ed. C.
Rossiter. New York: New American Library.

Markl, H.S. 1980. Report on group discussion. In
Morality as a biological phenomenon. Ed. G.S.
Stent. Berkeley: University of California Press.
————, H.S., ed. 1980a. Evolution of social behavior:
hypotheses and empirical tests. Weinheim: Verlag
Chemie.
Marshall, G. 1954. David Hume and political
scepticism. Philosophical Quarterly 4:247-257.
Masters, R. 1978. Of marmots and men: human altruism
and animal behavior. In Altruism, sympathy and
helping. Ed. L. Wispe New York: Academic Press,
pp. 59-77.
McClain, S. 1979. The political thought of the
Austrian School of Economics. Dissertation. Johns
Hopkins.
McCoy, D.R. 1980. The elusive republic: political
economy in Jeffersonian America. Chapel Hill:
University of North Carolina Press.
McIlwain, C. 1966. Constitutionalism ancient and
modern. Ithaca, N.Y.: Cornell University Press.
Medawar, P. 1982. Pluto's republic. New York: Oxford
University Press.
Medcalf, L. and Dolbeare, K. 1985. Neopolitics:
American political ideas in the 1980's. New York:
Random House.
Meiklejohn, D. 1978. Review of Law, legislation, and
liberty. Ethics 88:178-184.
————. 1980. Democracy and the rule of law. Ethics
91:117-124.
Merelman, R. 1984. Making something of ourselves.
Berkeley: University of California Press.
Merton, R.K. 1968. Social theory and social
structure. New York: Free Press.
Meyer, F.S. 1962. In defense of freedom: a
conservative credo. Chicago: Henry Regnery Co.
Meyers, M. 1981. The mind of the founder: sources of
the political thought of James Madison. Hanover:
University Press of New England.
Midgley, M. 1983. Toward a new understanding of human
nature: the limits of individualism. In How
humans adapt. A biocultural odyssey. Ed. D.
Ortner. Washington, D.C.: Smithsonian
Institution Press.
Miller, E. 1979. The cognitive basis of Hayek's
political thought. In Liberty and the rule of
law. Ed. R.L. Cunningham. College Station:
Texas A&M University Press.
Mitchell, W.C. 1983. Efficiency, responsibility, and
democratic politics. In Liberal democracy. Nomos,
no. 25. Yearbook of the American Society for
Political and Legal Philosophy. New York: New
York University Press.
Morgan, R.J. 1974. Madison's theory of representation

in the Tenth Federalist.   Journal of Politics
36:852-885.
————.   1981.   Madison's analysis of the sources of
political authority.   American Political Science
Review 75:613-625.
Mueller,   D.   1979.   Public   choice.   Cambridge:
Cambridge University Press.
Mulgan,   R.G.   1977.   Aristotle's political theory.
Oxford: Clarendon Press.
Nash,   G.H.   1976.   The   conservative   intellectual
movement in America.   New York: Basic Books.
Nash,   R.H.   1980.   Freedom,   justice and the state.
Washington, D.C.:   University Press of America.
Nisbet,   R.   1975.   Public opinion versus popular
opinion.   The Public Interest 41:166-192.
Nozick R.   1974.   Anarchy,   state,   and utopia.   New
York: Basic Books.
O'Brien,   D.P.   1975.   The   classical   economists.
Oxford: Clarendon Press.
O'Gorman,   F.   1973.   Edmund   Burke: his   political
philosophy.   Bloomington: Indiana   University
Press.
Orbell,   J.M.   and Wilson,   L.A.   1978.   Institutional
solutions to the n-prisoners' dilemma.   American
Political Science Review 72:411-421.
————.   1978a.   The   uses   of   expanded   majorities.
American Political Science Review 72:1366-1368.
Ostrom,   V.   1971.   The political theory of a compound
republic.   Blacksburg: Public   Choice   Center at
Virginia   Polytechnic   Institute   and   State   Uni-
versity.
O'Sullivan,   N.K.   1976.   Conservatism.   New York: St.
Martin's Press.
Padover,   S.K.   1953.   The complete Madison.   New York:
Harper.
Paley,   W.   1867.   The principles of moral and political
philosophy.   New York: Harper and Brothers.
Parekh,   B.   1982.   The political thought of Sir Isaiah
Berlin.   British   Journal   of   Political   Science
12:201-226.
Parkin,   C.   1956.   The moral basis of Burke's political
thought.   Cambridge: Cambridge University Press.
Parry,   G.   1982.   Tradition,   community,   and   self-
determination.   British   Journal   of   Political
Science 12:201-226.
Pennock,   J.R.   and   Chapman,   J.W.,   eds.   1979.
Constitutionalism.   Nomos,   No.   20.   Yearbook   of
the   American   Society   for   Political   and   Legal
Philosophy.   New York: New York University Press.
Pocock,   J.G.A.   1960.   Burke   and   the   ancient
constitution: a problem in the history of ideas.
Historical Journal 3:125-143.
————.   1972.   Virtue   and   commerce   in   the   18th

century.   Journal of Interdisciplinary History
3:119-134.
————.   1975.   The Machiavellian moment.   Princeton:
Princeton University Press.
————.   1982.   The   political   economy   of   Burke's
analysis of the French Revolution.   Historical
Journal 25:331-349.
Preece, R.   1980.   The political economy of Edmund
Burke.   Modern Age 24:266-273.
————.   1980.   Edmund   Burke   and   his   European
reception.   Eighteenth Century 21:255-273.
Preston, L.   1983.   Freedom and authority. Beyond the
precepts   of   liberalism.   American   Political
Science Review 77:666-674.
Purcell, E.A., Jr.   1973.   The crisis of democratic
theory.   Lexington: University Press
of Kentucky.
Quinton, A.   1978.   The politics of imperfection.
London: Faber and Faber.
Rawls, J.   1971.   A theory of justice.   Cambridge,
Mass.:   Harvard University Press.
————.   1980.   Kantian constructivism in moral theory:
the Dewey lectures 1980 Journal of Philosophy
77:515-572.
Raz, J.   1977.   The rule of law and its virtue.   Law
Quarterly Review 93:185-211.
Rees, J.C.   1963.   Hayek on liberty.   Philosophy
38:346-360.
Riemer, C.   1954.   The republicanism of James Madison.
Political Science Quarterly 69:45-64.
Robbins, L.C.   1963.   Hayek on liberty.   In Politics
and economics: papers in political economy.   Ed.
L.C. Robbins. New York: St. Martin's Press.
Rosenberg, N.   1960.   Some institutional aspects of the
Wealth of nations.   Journal of Political Economy
68:557-570.
Rothbard, M.N.   1982.   The ethics of liberty.   Atlantic
Highlands, N.J.: Humanities Press.
Ryan, C.   1976.   Yours, mine, and ours: property
rights and individual liberty.   Ethics 87:126-141.
Sabine, G.H.   1950.   Convention and tradition: Hume
and Burke.   In A history of political theory.   Ed.
G.H. Sabine. New York: H. Holt and Co.
Sandel, M.J.   1982.   Liberalism and the limits of
justice. New York: Cambridge University Press.
————, ed. 1984.   Liberalism and its critics.   New
York: New York University Press.
Sartori, G.   1962.   Constitutionalism: a preliminary
discussion.   American Political Science Review
56:853-864.
Scanlan, J.P.   1959.   The Federalist and human nature.
Review of Politics 21:657-677.
Schaefer, D.L.   1980.   Review of Law, legislation, and

liberty. Vol. 3: The political order of a free
people, by Friedrich A. Hayek. American Political
Science Review 74:165-166.
Schick, F. 1984. Having reasons: an essay on
rationality and sociality. Princeton: Princeton
University Press.
Schumacher, E.F. 1977. A guide for the perplexed.
New York: Harper and Row.
Seldon, A., ed. 1961. Agenda for a free society.
London: Hutchinson.
Selznick, P. 1949. TVA and the grass roots.
Berkeley: University of California Press.
Shenfield, A.A. 1976. The new thought of F.A. Hayek.
Modern Age 20:54-61.
Shils, E. 1981. Tradition. Chicago: University of
Chicago Press.
Spencer, M.E. 1978. Plato and the anatomy of
constitutions. Social theory and practice
5:95-130.
Stanlis, P. 1961. The basis of Burke's political
conservatism. Modern Age 5:263-274.
————. 1974. A preposterous way of reasoning:
Dreyer's Edmund Burke: the philospher in action.
Studies in Burke and His Time 15:265-277.
Stewart, J.B. 1963. The moral and political
philosophy of David Hume. New York: Columbia
University Press.
Streissler, E., ed. 1969. Roads to freedom: essays
in honour of Friedrich A. von Hayek. New York:
Augustus M. Kelley.
Taylor, M. 1982. Community, anarchy and liberty.
Cambridge: Cambridge University Press.
Taylor, O.H. 1955. Economics and liberalism.
Cambridge: Harvard University Press.
Troy, F.S. 1981. Edmund Burke and the break with
tradition. Massachusetts Review 22:93-132.
Tucker, R., ed. 1978. The Marx-Engels reader. New
York: W.W. Norton and Company, Inc.
Vanberg, V. 1986. Spontaneous market order and social
rules. Economics and Philosophy 2:75-100.
Vaughn, K.I. 1982. Can democratic society reform
itself: the limits of constructive change. Paper
presented to Mont Pelerin Society, September.
Vernon, R. 1976. The Great Society and the Open
Society: liberalism in Hayek and Popper.
Canadian Journal of Political Science 9:261-276.
Vile, M.J.C. 1961. Constitutionalism and the
separation of powers. Oxford: Clarendon Press.
Vine, I. 1983. The nature of moral commitments. In
Morality in the Making. Ed. H. Weinreich-Haste
and D. Locke. New York: John Wiley and Sons.
Viner, J. 1961. Hayek on freedom and coercion.
Southern Economic Journal 27:230-236.

Waligorski, C.   1984.   Conservative economist critics
   of democracy. Social Science Journal 21:99-116.
Ward, B.   1979.   The ideal worlds of economics.   New
   York: Basic Books.
Watkins, J.W.N.   1961.   Philosophy.   In Agenda for a
   free society.   Ed.   A.   Seldon.   London:
   Hutchinson.
Weston, J.C., Jr.   1961.   Edmund Burke's view of
   history. Review of Politics 23:203-229.
Wilhelm, M.   1972.   The political thought of Friedrich
   A. Hayek. Political Studies 20:169-184.
Wilkins, B.T.   1967.   The problem of Burke's political
   philosophy. Oxford: Clarendon Press.
Wills, G.   1981.   Explaining America: The Federalist.
   Garden City, N.Y.: Doubleday and Company.
Winch, D.   1978.   Adam Smith's politics.   Cambridge:
   Cambridge University Press.
Winston, K.   1983.   Toward   a   liberal   theory   of
   legislation.   In Liberal democracy.   Nomos, no.
   25.   Yearbook of the American Society for Pol-
   itical and Legal Philosophy. New York: New York
   University Press.
Wolff, P.H.   1980.   The biology of morals from a
   psychological perspective.   In Morality as a
   biological phenomenon. Ed. G.S. Stent. Berkeley:
   University of California Press.
Wolin, S.   1954.   Hume and conservatism.   American
   Political Science Review 48:999-1016.
────.   1960.   Politics and vision. Boston: Little,
   Brown.
────.   1969.   Political   theory   as   a   vocation.
   American Political Science Review 63:1062-1082.
Wood, G.S.   1969.   Representation in the American
   Revolution.   Charlottesville: University   of
   Virginia Press.

Index

About the Author

BARBARA M. ROWLAND is an Assistant Professor of Political Science at Northern Arizona University and was formerly an Assistant Professor of Political Science at Colorado State University. Professor Rowland received her Ph.D. in political science from the University of Oregon in 1983.